1-2-3

Annuities

Discover how they work,
Discuss their pros and cons,
Decide if they're for you

Steve Lewit · Gabriel Lewit

1 – 2 – 3 Annuities:

Discover How They Work,
Discuss Their Pros and Cons,
Decide If They're for You

© 1-2-3 Annuities LLC

This publication is designed to provide accurate and authoritative information with regard to the subject matter covered. It is sold with the understanding that the publisher is not engaged in rendering legal, accounting, or other professional advice. If legal advice or other expert assistance is required it, the services of a competent professional should be sought.

The information in this book is for general use and, while we believe the information is reliable and accurate, it is important to remember individual situations may be entirely different.

Therefore, information should be relied upon only when coordinated with individual professional tax and/or financial advice. You need to consider your specific financial situation including your health and legacy goals before acting on any information presented in this book. Please note that neither the information presented, nor any opinion expressed is to be considered as an offer to buy or purchase any insurance or securities products and services referenced in this book. All information contained is for educational purposes only.

All figures and examples in this book are based on rates and assumptions as of the dates shown in each example. Rates and assumptions are not guaranteed and may be subject to change. As in all assumptions and examples, individual results may vary based on a wide range of factors unique to each person's situation. All data provided in this book are to be used for informational purposes only. Any slights against individuals, companies, or organizations are unintentional.

*For those who wish
to learn, understand,
and live a richer life.*

CONTENTS

Foreword

After a combined 42 years of working with people who are either planning for or are already in retirement, we've found that annuities top the list of the most misunderstood, misrepresented, and misused products in the financial industry. When the subject of annuities, especially Fixed Index Annuities (FIAs), comes up in conversations with clients, it's not uncommon to hear them say things like:

"Oh, I heard they are horrible!"

"Why would I want to buy something with so many fees?"

"I was told to never buy an annuity."

Or even: "Are you kidding me? Everyone is trying to sell me an annuity. No way!"

Once understood, however, annuities are a good fit for many retirement plans. As a result, their rate of acceptance and growth has consistently accelerated, perhaps faster than any other financial product.

Our interest in these products started back in 1995 when the first Fixed Index Annuities appeared on the market. To us, they sounded too good to be true. Over the years, however, we've discovered that

they perform efficiently and reliably. Due to their consistent performance and research findings from industry leaders such as Morningstar, Ibbotson, and the Financial Research Corporation, many investors have included annuities (most notably Fixed Index Annuities) as a
valuable component of their financial plans. Yet, "too good to be true"
is still a comment we hear quite often.

What is it that causes doubt about annuities? Why, after so many
years of success and popularity, are they still viewed with mistrust?
How can we give consumers the objective facts about annuities and
the financial strategies that incorporate them? These are the questions
we have asked ourselves. The solution turned out to be *1-2-3 Annuities*.

In the last decade, Fixed Annuity offerings have consistently
delivered new, more effective, and more flexible benefits, all of which
have contributed to their growing popularity. At the same time,
however, a body of literature, commentary, and advertising with a
negative bias also grew. Like all products, Fixed Annuities have their
own set of pros and cons. Those who held (and still hold) a negative
bias either don't understand annuities or misrepresent them, often to
protect their own interests. *1-2-3 Annuities* was written to cut through
this noise and provide simple, candid, and objective information about
this product class.

In *1-2-3 Annuities*, we've incorporated a great deal about the nuts
and bolts of annuities, but you will also find a range of different
annuity uses and strategies, each targeted to best serve your personal
planning objectives, investment style, age, and emotional makeup.
These strategies, combined with a deeper understanding of how
annuities work, will give you a solid decision-making foundation,
empowering you to make wise decisions about these products.

We hope that *1-2-3 Annuities* will be a valuable ally, making your pre-retirement and retirement journey more confident, secure, and fulfilling.

— Steve Lewit & Gabriel Lewit

Introduction

People worry!

When it comes to saving and accumulating money, especially money for retirement, people worry a lot. After all, what could be worse than running out of money during the years that are supposed to be some of the best of your life?

Should people worry so much about their retirement? You bet. The future is an unknown, and in today's political and economic environment, the unknown is as unpredictable as ever. Most people eventually ask themselves these important questions concerning retirement: Will I be okay? Will I have enough to pay for healthcare? Will Social Security be enough? Will I lose big in the market? Will inflation eat up the value of my money? Will taxes rise, leaving me less to spend? Will I live too long and run out of money altogether? All questions which, unanswered, can make us anxious about the future.

It's simple; most people just don't like the unknown. Annuities were created to minimize or eliminate the unknown, especially about the safety of your investments and future income. Their growing popularity is a direct result of their ability to make the unknown more predictable, safer, and more secure, enabling you to approach your financial future with confidence, hope, and peace of mind.

Are annuities a good choice for you? Can they help you meet your financial goals? Will they give you a greater sense of security about the future? We don't know, but that's the purpose of *1-2-3 Annuities*. Our book will help you extricate yourself from all the conflicting information and opinions that circulate about annuities. It will provide you with accurate information, minus the bias and hyperbole, and with your welfare—not market share—in mind.

1-2-3 Annuities has Three Major Sections:

Discover

This section is about understanding how annuities work and where they fit into a financial plan. Here you'll get a chance to crack open the case and see what makes these products tick. If you're the kind of person who sees a watch and wants to study the inner workings, this section will work for you, but it may not be as granular as you would prefer. On the other hand, if you are a person who just wants a good-looking watch that tells time accurately, but you aren't too concerned with the cogs and gears, you will find this section works for you too, giving you a solid basis in the inner workings of annuities while allowing you to skip over the more technical details.

Discuss

This section examines how annuities can be used to reach specific goals and answers the most common questions from consumers. Here you will find clear and accurate explanations of the pros and cons of annuities, as well as the aspects that may work for or against your financial goals. Our aim for "Discuss" is to give you an open and honest forum that builds on "Discover" and sets the foundation for the next section, "Decide."

Decide

Is an annuity right for you? How much should you put into an annuity? How do you choose the right one? What's the best way to purchase an annuity? And what other financial pieces do you need in place before you make that purchase? This section will answer these questions.

Most of us are not great decision makers, and when we do finally decide, those decisions are often peppered with anxiety and second-guessing. When we make bigger decisions about investments or retirement income, emotions rise to a higher level and we are often left thinking, "Geez, I sure hope I did the right thing!"

This section will arm you with simple and precise steps you can take to satisfy both your financial and emotional goals. It will help you make—and commit—to a decision about purchasing an annuity. "Decide" is intended to minimize your self-doubt so you can continue your financial and life journey with ease and assurance.

That's it!

"Discover," "Discuss," "Decide." Take one section at a time and let's see if annuities belong in your financial future.

DISCOVER

The Discover section is your first step towards understanding the meaning, purpose and inner workings of annuities and where annuities may fit into your financial plan. It will also help uncover your Unique Annuity Mindset— the way you think and feel about annuities.

Every investment option, and there are many, has its pros and cons, serves a specific purpose, and comes with different levels of complexity. Annuities are one of these options and they can be a bit complex. In this section we aim to provide a clear understanding of the workings of the most important aspects of annuities and how they may fit into your planning needs. Annuities, like all things, are not for everyone.

This section provides a comprehensive, factual education of annuities. The following section, *Discuss*, builds on your understanding of these facts. The *Discover* and *Discuss* sections then form the basis for the final section, *Decision*, where you will choose whether to use annuities in your financial plan.

Your Unique Annuity Mindset

Every person has a Unique Annuity Mindset, the sum of their perceptions and experiences about annuities as gathered from advertising, financial commentary, books, and newsletters, Google searches, and popular financial TV show hosts. Today, your Unique Annuity Mindset is probably more powerful than you realize and can have a meaningful impact—either positive or negative—on your annuity buying decision.

For example, many people have immediate negative reactions to annuities even though they have never been taught how they work and what they can do. That negativity is their Unique Annuity Mindset in action. Their Mindset hears the word "annuity" and it is immediately filled with negativity, negativity which is based on some truths, some half-truths and some information that is entirely false.

Sometimes a person's Unique Annuity Mindset is so negative they discard the idea of learning about annuities altogether, losing what might have been a great financial opportunity. Everyone has a Unique Annuity Mindset. So, as you read each chapter of *1-2-3 Annuities*, your

Unique Annuity Mindset may jump in, for example, and say things like:

"I agree with that."

"That's not what I heard."

"That sounds too good to be true!"

"My advisor told me something else."

"I know someone who got screwed when he bought an annuity."

"Oh, I don't believe that."

To begin our journey, let's see if we can get a better understanding of how you currently think about annuities. By understanding your Unique Annuity Mindset today, and seeing your biases clearly, your reading of *1-2-3 Annuities* will be more objective, productive, enjoyable and financially rewarding.

What Is Your Unique Annuity Mindset?

Read the following statements and rank your agreement from 1 – 5, where 1 means you strongly disagree, and 5 means you strongly agree.

Your Unique Annuity Mindset	Ranking
I would never buy an annuity	1 2 3 4 5
Annuities are laden with fees	1 2 3 4 5
Annuities lock up your money	1 2 3 4 5
When you die, the insurance company keeps your money	1 2 3 4 5
Annuities are too good to be true	1 2 3 4 5
Annuities over-promise and under-deliver	1 2 3 4 5

The return on annuities is so low, you can barely beat inflation	1	2	3	4	5
It's not worth trading higher growth potential for zero losses	1	2	3	4	5
Annuities are too complicated to understand	1	2	3	4	5
I've heard so many conflicting things about annuities, I just won't buy one.	1	2	3	4	5
TOTAL SCORE					

What Is Your Unique Annuity Mindset – Scoring:

10 – 20   **Extremely Positive Annuity Mindset**

Annuities are right up your alley and may be the answer to achieving many of your financial goals. At the same time, however, you are not naïve. Your Unique Annuity Mindset, despite your positive bias, has led you to do your due diligence by reading *1-2-3 Annuities*. As you read this book, keep your positive bias in mind. Sometimes, a positive bias can work against you as much as a negative bias by blurring the truth, causing you to see only the benefits of annuities because you don't want to hear anything negative to upset your viewpoint. As you read *1-2-3 Annuities*, allow yourself to consider each point from both positive and negative perspectives. Don't let your Unique Annuity Mindset skew your consideration by filtering out aspects of annuities that are important, but unsavory.

21 – 30   **Positive Annuity Mindset**

You have a positive bias toward annuities. Your Unique Annuity Mindset, however, has heard and seen enough about the drawbacks of annuities that you wonder if your positive bias is justified. Your bias drives you to learn more about these products. You've heard they can be a helpful addition to your investment portfolio and you like what you've heard. Because of your positive bias, you hope that reading *1-2-3 Annuities* will give you the insight and understanding necessary to solidify your positive feelings about annuities and make your decision to purchase an annuity as comfortable and confident as possible. If you begin to come around to the idea of purchasing an annuity, your Unique Annuity Mindset may make you feel the need to sell yourself on the merits of annuities every time you turn the page.

| 31 –40 | **Negative Annuity Mindset** |

While past experiences may have given you a negative bias toward annuities, you have heard enough positives to consider them in your financial planning, which is probably why you are reading this book. However, your Unique Annuity Mindset will likely be an ongoing challenge. Even if you decide to purchase an annuity, you may find major doubts creeping into your decision. You might catch yourself wondering:

"Why on earth did I buy this?"

"Was I duped into believing an annuity would be good for me?"

"Did I make a big mistake I can't fix?"

Be aware that it will probably take considerable determination and self-awareness to sort through your misgivings and fully embrace your decision.

| 41 – 50 | **Extremely Negative Annuity Mindset** |

When it comes to annuities, you have a strong negative bias. While you are willing to consider them, your Unique Annuity Mindset may be too strong, holding too much negative sway over your decision to employ an annuity in your financial plans. As you read *1-2-3 Annuities*, you may find yourself focusing on your doubts rather than the fact that an annuity might serve you well. If you pay attention to these apprehensions as they arise and consider how they undermine your ability to see annuities objectively, you may find yourself more open to using this product class than you expect.

As we move along in *1-2-3 Annuities*, you will get a deeper understanding of your Unique Annuity Mindset, how it affects your opinions and decisions, and what you can do to be more objective. Let's begin our exploration by taking a broader view of where annuities fit into the world of financial products.

Where Do Annuities Fit In?

Red Money Products are Market-based

Principal is *not guaranteed*

Green Money Products are Insurance-based

Principal is *guaranteed*

Investors are presented with many investment options, products, and strategies. Product options fall into two categories, Red and Green. The color of each does not mean that one is better or worse than the other. Red does not equal bad and Green does not equal good, even though we often associate those qualities with these colors.

In this context, Red simply means you are investing in products that carry the risk of loss, while Green indicates that a product is free from the risk of market loss. There is nothing inherently "good" or "bad" in these product choices; one product may be a good choice for one person and bad for another. All products have their pros and cons and each must be considered in relation to your Unique Annuity Mindset and financial goals.

For example, if you are a person who can tolerate risk, you have undoubtedly leaned toward using Red Products in the past and will probably continue to lean that way in the future. You understand that to reap the rewards of higher gains you must take greater risk. You are comfortable with investments that are variable, indeterminate, and somewhat unpredictable.

On the other hand, if you're the type of person who does not like putting your money at risk of loss in the market, you have probably placed more of your funds in Green Products and you will probably lean that way in the future. Because you are risk-averse, you are willing to sacrifice potential growth to eliminate potential loss. You prefer a financial future that is more predictable and less variable, ultimately granting you a greater sense of stability and peace of mind.

Over the years, financial professionals representing both Red and Green Products have fought each other, both claiming that their products are superior while, at the same time, trying desperately to protect their market share and profit margins. Although that battle continues today, an increasing number of financial professionals recognize the wisdom of using both Red and Green Products to help you reach your financial goals.

These professionals are willing to consider both equities and annuities, for example, with an objective focus on which product is better for you, rather than which is better in theory. In a later chapter we'll take a closer look at how you can determine the appropriate Red and Green allocations for your investments. Most importantly, we'll examine your Green options, where annuities are a major player.

Red and Green Product Overview

Red Products are investments that put your money at risk of loss. Products in the Red category are all market-based and include: Stocks, Bonds, Mutual Funds, Commodities, REITs, Managed Futures, Variable Annuities and Variable Life Insurance.

Stocks Bonds Mutual Funds	Commodities REITs Managed Futures	Variable Annuities	Variable Life Insurance

"Red" product values are controlled by market forces and rise and fall based on the supply and demand of the trading community.

With market-based products, their value is always determined by market forces and rise and fall based on the supply and demand of the trading community. When there are more sellers than buyers, values fall; and, when there are more buyers than sellers, values rise. Sometimes, when the sellers want to sell at a faster rate than buyers want to buy, values fall rapidly, much like they did the seventeen month period from October 2007 through March 2009, when the market dropped -56.4%. Likewise, markets can skyrocket when buyers buy faster than sellers sell. In the very next year, 2009, the S&P 500 rebounded 23.5%, erasing some of the prior year's losses. All Red Products carry risk, some higher and more volatile, some lower and less volatile.

All Green Products are principal-guaranteed, meaning you will never lose money because of market changes. Products in this category are generally backed by the government or insurance companies and include: Money Market, Savings, Treasuries, CDs, Fixed Interest Annuities, and Fixed Index Annuities.

Money Market Savings	Treasuries CDs Fixed Interest Annuities	Fixed Index Annuities	Indexed Universal Life Insurance

"Green" products are principal-guaranteed, which means you cannot lose your "principal" funds—the money you put into the account

The principal deposited into these products is insured against loss, which is why they are often called "safe money" products. Unlike Red Products, Green Products offer stability, making the future more predictable and promoting peace of mind for the risk-averse investor.

Remember, there is no such thing as a perfect product. They all have their pros and cons, components which work better or which you like better, and other components that work less well or which you like less well. As a matter of principle, any product you choose should be chosen for one—and only one—reason; because it is the best product to help you reach your financial goals, no matter which color it happens to be.

When products are purchased on their merits and their ability to help you achieve your goals, the probability of financial success is much higher. As we said earlier, there are rarely bad products, but there are certainly products that are bad for you! Our focus in this book is annuities. So, let's jump in and take a closer look.

Annuities

Annuities come in two core varieties—Variable and Fixed, which are Red and Green respectively. Funds invested in Variable Annuities are invested in the market through sub-accounts, which are basically mutual funds, and their values rise and fall with the market.

Fixed Annuities, on the other hand, are not invested in the market and are therefore not subject to market losses. All Fixed Annuities are principal-guaranteed products that grow at a specified rate or an indexed rate (more about this later). In both cases, funds deposited into a Fixed Annuity are insured against loss by the claims-paying ability of the insurance carrier.

For *1-2-3 Annuities*, we chose to focus on Fixed Annuities for three reasons:

1. A book about both Variable and Fixed Annuities, because of its necessary length and breadth of content might be off-putting and too much for one book to cover.

2. Based on current industry research, our own research, and years of experience helping people plan for retirement, we believe that Fixed Annuities are a more efficient and less expensive product class.

3. Industry trends document the declining popularity of Variable Annuities and the growing popularity of Fixed Annuities, especially Fixed Index Annuities.

With that distinction in mind, let's dive in!

The Three Types of Fixed Annuities

Immediate Annuities (IA)

Fixed Interest Annuities (MYGA)

Fixed Index Annuities (FIA)

The three types of Fixed Annuities

Fixed Annuities fall into three product categories: Immediate, Fixed Interest, and Fixed Index. All these annuities are built to satisfy someone that leans toward guaranteed principal, reasonable growth rates, and/or guaranteed income. The world of Fixed Annuities is also a world of broad variety and complexity, offering a vast array of products. When you first begin to explore Fixed Annuities, don't be surprised if your mind feels challenged at almost every turn. In fact, many of the strategic uses of these products will trigger the suspicion that they are just too good to be true.

As you will see, however, Fixed Annuities offer options and possibilities that foster confidence, security, and a higher quality of life well into the future. But before we dive deeper into each Fixed Annuity category, let's get some overall annuity basics out of the way.

Fixed Annuity Basic Facts

Fixed Annuities are like ice cream. They come in assorted flavors and you can add many kinds of features. They also have certain basic ingredients that we've outlined here:

Fixed Annuity Basic Facts
1 CONTRACT & TERM   Annuities are a Contract between you and an insurance company. Many are designed for a specific number of years called the surrender period, contract period, or term of the annuity.
2 WITHDRAWAL OPTIONS   With exception of Immediate Annuities, you can withdraw your funds from an annuity at any time after the first year. Typically, you will receive your funds within 10 business days of the request. During the contract period, however, you will incur additional charges if you withdraw funds over and above a stated annual limit (usually 5% or 10%). These additional charges are called surrender charges and normally decrease each year of the contract period. If you withdraw funds prior to 59 ½ you will incur tax penalties.
3 GUARANTEES   Annuities are guaranteed by the claims-paying ability of the issuing insurance company. Historically, insurance companies have an impeccable record of safety, even in instances when the company gets into financial difficulty (it doesn't happen that often, but it does happen).
4 NO OR LOW FEES   Some Fixed Annuities have fees and some don't. As we will explore later, it often depends on what features you add to your annuity. The determining factor for choosing an annuity is not whether it has fees, but whether it's the best product to help you meet your goals.

5 ENHANCED BENEFITS / RIDERS

Many annuities offer enhanced benefits or contract "riders" such as for income, health care, nursing care, terminal illness, and bonuses, although these additions may come at an additional cost or fee.

6 TAX-DEFERRAL

All annuities are tax-deferred. When funds are withdrawn, interest is withdrawn first and taxed as ordinary income. Principal is not taxed when it is withdrawn (unless it is from an IRA or another qualified retirement account).

7 ROLLOVERS & TRANSFERS

IRA, 401(k), 403(b), TSA, SEP, Roth, TSP, and all other retirement plans can typically be rolled into an annuity without any tax consequences.

8 SURRENDER SCHEDULE & DEATH BENEFIT

Fixed Annuities have a cost or surrender charge associated with the annuity if you want to do a full liquidation or full transfer of the funds out of the annuity during the specified term of the annuity contract. However, upon death, all surrender charges are eliminated and money passed to your heirs as a lump-sum or installments or payments.

9 FREE LOOK PERIOD

All Fixed Annuities have a free look period of 15 to 30 days from the time you receive your annuity contract. During this time you may rescind your contract and have all your funds returned to you (usually within 10 business days).

10 GROWTH & INTEREST EARNINGS

For most Fixed Annuities, interest is credited once a year on the anniversary date of the annuity (the date your annuity was funded). How much interest is based on a Crediting Method, which we will explore in a later chapter.

Overview of Each Type of Fixed Annuity

Let's look at a high-level overview of the different types of Fixed Annuities. As we move along, keep in mind that in later chapters we will explore the different strategies and applications of Fixed Annuities in greater detail, where some of the questions you may have now will be answered.

Immediate Annuities (IA)

Immediate Annuities are for people who are totally focused on income. They are strictly for generating a lifetime income stream and serve no other purpose.

When investors hear the word "annuity," this is often the type of annuity that comes to mind. In an Immediate Annuity you make a lump-sum payment to the insurance company which, in exchange, guarantees you a specific amount of monthly or annual income for the rest of your life. In technical words, this is called "annuitizing" your policy.

Any time your hear the word "annuitize" with regard to income distribution from an annuity, it means that you pass control of your principal to the insurance company in exchange for lifetime guaranteed income. All Immediate Annuities use annuitization as the method of providing income. Deferred Annuities, which we will take a closer look at later, means the income is deferred to a point of time in the future. At that time, you can also annuitize the annuity in the same way as you would an Immediate Annuity.

However, as you will soon see, more modern annuities provide an alternative income route using an Income Rider, where your principal remains under your control, but you still receive guaranteed lifetime income.

You may be familiar with Immediate Annuities because it is the kind that Mom and Dad or Grandma and Grandpa purchased years ago. You may have heard them say that when they die the insurance company keeps the remaining funds. When the conversation turns to annuities, it's not uncommon to hear people say something like, "Oh, that's where you give your money to the insurance company and never get it back, right? Why would anyone want to do that?" But that assessment applies only to income from annuitization and is not totally accurate.

You can guarantee, even when annuitizing your policy, that you will get some money back, albeit via income rather than a lump sum. Let's make sure we understand how these products work. You want immediate income. You deposit $100,000 with XYZ Insurance Company which then guarantees you $6,300 annually with "10 years certain" by annuitizing the policy. The "10 years certain" means that if you died six years after purchasing your annuity, the insurance company would continue to pay your heirs for four more years, yielding a total of 10.

After the 10-year certain period, payments would stop and the insurance company would keep any remaining funds. If you live longer than 10 years, income would continue beyond the 10-year certain period for the remainder of your life.

There are different certainty-periods you can choose from, i.e. a 5-year period certain, 10-year period certain, or even 20-year period certain. However, the more years you guarantee with a certainty period, the less your guaranteed income payment amount will be each year.

Lump Sum to Insurance Company

Period Certain Income
Income is guaranteed to you, your spouse or your heirs for a specific period of time i.e. 10 years.

Income continues for a Lifetime
But ceases upon death (if a joint payout, then income will cease when the surviving spouse dies). Nothing left for heirs.

Fixed Interest Annuities (MYGA)

Fixed Interest Annuities, or as they are often called, Multi-Year Guaranteed Annuities (MYGAs) are similar to CDs (Bank issued Certificates of Deposit), which is why they appeal to people that like using CDs as a safe way to earn interest. These same investors think of MYGAs as CDs on steroids because MYGAs, like CDs, guarantee a specific amount of interest over a set time period but usually at higher rates. People with a CD orientation usually find that MYGAs are a good fit and that the transition from CD to MYGA an easy adjustment.

MYGAs are simple to understand. For example, you could purchase a five-year MYGA that guarantees 4.00% interest each year for five years. Should you decide to take your money out of the MYGA prior to the end of the five-year period, as with a CD, a penalty or surrender charge may be applied. However, unlike a CD, where earned interest is taxed each year, interest earned in annuities is tax-deferred—you only pay taxes on interest when funds are withdrawn from the annuity.

Immediate and Fixed Interest Annuities (MYGAs) are the simplest annuity types. They are easy to understand, with few moving parts and typically carry no annual fees.

Lump Sum to Insurance Company

Funds grow at a specific guaranteed interest rate for the term of the contract, e.g. 4% each year for 5 years.

Fixed Index Annuities (FIA)

Fixed Index Annuities are uniquely designed annuity products which entered the scene in 1995 when Keyport Life introduced the first equity-linked Index Annuity called the KeyIndex annuity. Since then their popularity has grown considerably, but as we have said, they remain widely misunderstood and misrepresented. FIAs are suitable for individuals seeking safe growth or a combination of safe growth, income, and asset preservation.

Unlike Variable Annuities, where your funds are invested directly in the market via sub-account mutual funds, Fixed Index Annuities link your money to a market index such as the S&P 500 using a mathematical formula called a Crediting Strategy. This formula determines how much interest will be credited to your annuity as the associated index rises and falls.

Fixed Index Annuity (FIA) — Funds are linked to the market by a mathematical formula called a Crediting or Index Strategy

While there are many kinds of Crediting Strategies, most have these two core features:

- When the market and the corresponding index rise, interest is credited to your annuity, typically up to a certain limit or cap.
- When the market and the corresponding index fall, whether its -5%, -25% or -50%, there are no losses in your annuity account.

This may be your first "too good to be true" moment. People often say, "You mean I can get market gains but never worry about losing money when the market crashes?" While it may sound too good to be true, that's basically what happens—but there are some important details to understand.

Here's an example. Let's say the Crediting Strategy for your Fixed Index Annuity has an annual cap of 5.5% and is linked to the S&P 500 index. Over the year, the S&P 500 rises 8%. Since the FIA is capped at 5.5% and the S&P 500 rose beyond that level, the maximum interest (5.5%) is credited to your account value. In FIA terms, we would say that the annuity "capped out" that year at 5.5%.

+ 8%

+ 5.5% (Cap Rate)

FIA with 5.5% Annual Point-to-Point Cap
in a rising market (the S&P 500)

FIA Accumulation,
Cash,
or Account Value

CREDITING STRATEGY

Stock Market Index
(such as the S&P 500)

If the S&P had risen only 3%, the full 3% would be credited to your account value because it falls below the 5.5% index cap.

The second core feature of most Fixed Index Annuities is that there are no losses when the market goes down. In other words, when interest is earned each year that gain—and the new, higher annuity value—is "locked in" and can never be lost. If the market declines, there is no change in the value of the FIA.

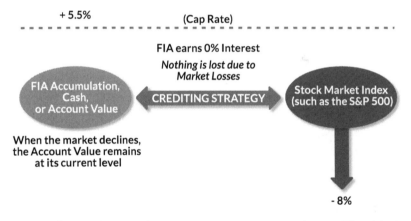

+ 5.5% (Cap Rate)

FIA earns 0% Interest

*Nothing is lost due to
Market Losses*

FIA Accumulation,
Cash,
or Account Value

CREDITING STRATEGY

Stock Market Index
(such as the S&P 500)

When the market declines,
the Account Value remains
at its current level

- 8%

In the illustration on the next page you can see how a Fixed Index Annuity grows. As the market and linked index rise each year, interest is being earned and credited to the annuity. That gain is then locked in and can never be lost. This is called an Annual Reset. When the market and linked index fall the locked in value stays the same. When the market rises again, interest is earned yet again.

In other words, in an FIA you never are in a position where you

When the market rises, interest is earned.
When the market falls, nothing is lost.

FIA
Initial Deposit
$500,000

Gains are always locked in.

Stock Market Index
(such as theS&P 500)

How FIAs work

have to recoup losses as you would if your money were invested directly in the market.

Many Fixed Index Annuities offer an additional component that provides a guaranteed lifetime income—income you cannot outlive. Unlike Immediate Annuities, where income begins immediately via annuitizing the policy, many FIAs defer income to a future date and provide income through an Income Rider, a benefit which is added to the base policy.

When you hear the words "Deferred Annuity" or "Deferred Income Annuity," it means the income is delayed and does not begin immediately. When the income is then created via the Income Rider instead of annuitization, you keep control of your principal. We'll take a much closer look at Income Riders in a later chapter. For now let's keep it simple and understand that FIAs that offer deferred income have two phases: an accumulation phase and an income or payout phase

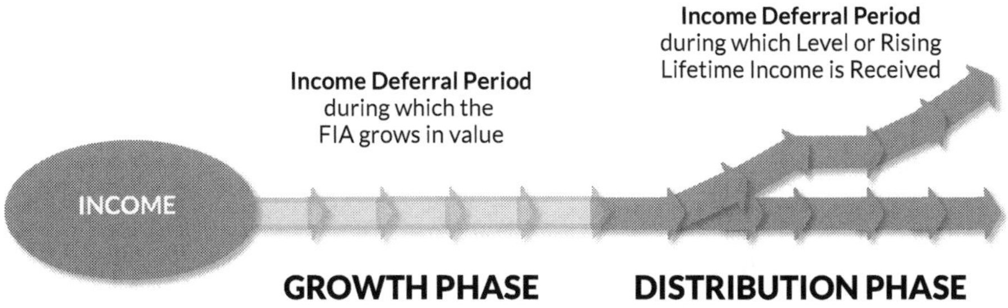

Income Deferral Period
during which the
FIA grows in value

Income Deferral Period
during which Level or Rising
Lifetime Income is Received

INCOME

GROWTH PHASE   **DISTRIBUTION PHASE**

Phases of a Deferred Income Annuity

These three types of annuities—Immediate, Multi-Year Guaranteed, and Fixed Index—can all satisfy the part of a person's mindset which seeks greater predictability and safety in his or her portfolio.

Growth Without Risk

Whether you know it or not, your Unique Annuity Mindset has already embraced annuities. In fact, you've already purchased one.

How could that be?

The word "annuity" can be applied to any kind of insurance or investment that entitles you to a series of guaranteed annual payments for a specific time period, or more usually, for life. Virtually all payments that are guaranteed for a set period or a lifetime fall under this definition. As a result, you are familiar with many annuity payments but have probably never thought of them as annuities. These are some examples of common annuity payments:

- Social Security
- Pensions
- Structured settlements
- Lottery winnings paid out with the lifetime payment option

Social Security contributions are deducted from each paycheck you receive. Those funds go to purchase your Social Security annuity.

If you are retired, you may already be receiving these annuity payments (Social Security). Pensions are similar but are purchased by you or for you by your employer. If you like the idea of getting guaranteed income deposited into your bank account every month, then your mind has already developed an implicit desire for annuities.

Now, you're reading this book. Why? Did you hear about annuities on TV or radio? Perhaps you went to a dinner seminar and an insurance agent was trying to sell you one? Did you read something positive (or negative) about them that captured your attention? Maybe a friend told you to never buy one—or told you that you should buy one, carrying on about how great it was to get income every month, worry-free? Regardless, something in your mind has driven you to explore annuities and to read this book. Suddenly you are on a mission to discover if an annuity will serve you well!

When it comes to annuities, there are two potential core objectives:

Annuity Objective #1
Growth Without Risk

Annuity Objective #2
Income Without Risk

In this chapter, we are going to focus on Growth Without Risk.

The Growth Without Risk Objective

If this is your goal, you are a person seeking to grow your assets with the least amount of risk or, preferably, no risk at all.

Traditionally, you have kept a portion of your assets in CDs, treasuries, savings accounts, and/or investment-grade bonds. While some people with the objective of Growth Without Risk believe bonds are a safe investment, they also understand that bonds are not 100% principal-guaranteed and can lose value in the market. Therefore, they often shy away from bonds as a suitable growth-without-risk option.

Why Do People Start Seeking Growth Without Risk?

- **You are becoming more conservative as you grow older.**

    They say age brings wisdom. You have matured and recognize that you are entering a new phase of life, moving from the accumulation stage, when you were buying and saving for the future, into the decumulation or distribution stage when you must generate your income from retirement savings.

    Today, as you get closer to retirement, you still want your assets to grow, but with greater safety so you can be confident that your assets will be there to produce income when you are retired and no longer earning a salary.

- **You realize that as you age you have less time to recoup losses.**

    You have invested in the market and over the years you've been through its ups and downs. You have also made mistakes— poor stock or mutual fund selection, trying to time the market and missing badly, or following the "hot" newsletter only to find out it was cold. You also know that when the market drops (as it did in 2000, 2001, and 2008), it may take five to six years to recoup your losses (if you didn't panic and sell when you saw the value of your investments plummet).

Finally, you've learned that if you do get caught in a down market, you will need to sell stocks or mutual funds to create income or withdraw required minimum distributions (RMDs) when values are low—only to have fewer remaining assets to recoup losses when the market recovers. You know that when you are in or near your retirement, time is not on your side if you lose money.

- **You are naturally risk-averse or have a visceral dislike of losing money.**

    Some people just don't like taking risks. It is built into their DNA. If that's you, then you would probably describe yourself as a conservative investor. After all the hard work of saving and accumulating assets during your working years, losing money often causes strong emotional reactions—anger, disappointment, suspicion of others, regret, stress, and worry.

    If you have money in the market when the market falls, you're they type of person who can't explain it away as a "paper loss" as many advisors suggest. You see it differently. Before the market fell you were worth X, but now you are worth Y and Y is far less than X, paper loss be damned! The money you worked so hard to accumulate is (for the time being) gone, and no one likes to lose money.

    The difference between you and a true risk-taker is that the risk-taker's adrenaline spikes when the markets are volatile and they have a sense of enjoyment and challenge alongside the anger and fear. Risk takers embrace these feelings as part of the investing experience while you prefer to eliminate them.

Whatever it is that drives your objective of Growth Without Risk, the problem you face today is that traditional safe-haven products such as CDs, treasuries, and savings accounts offer some of the lowest interest rates in history, often earning returns that barely keep up with inflation, if at all.

At the end of the day, deposits in these accounts, in inflation adjusted dollars, are essentially a losing proposition. By default, you turn toward annuities to see if there are better opportunities. When you do, you will find two primary annuity products which may serve you well—MYGAs and FIAs.

1. Multi-Year Guaranteed Annuity (MYGA)

As we saw earlier, Multi-Year Guaranteed Annuities are very much like CDs in that they guarantee a specific annual interest rate for an established time period. Today, 4/22/2019, for example, you could purchase a five-year CD guaranteed at 3.15 % per year for five years. On the other hand, you could purchase a five-year MYGA that will pay 4.0 % over the same period.

To get a higher interest rate in either a CD or an MYGA, you would have to extend the holding period, e.g. 10 years rather than five. However, in today's interest rate environment, the rate will only be marginally higher and may not be worth the longer time commitment.

When comparing CDs and MYGAs keep in mind that interest on CDs (unless IRA qualified) is taxable each year it is earned, whether you take it out of the CD or leave it in. Unlike CDs however, multi-year guaranteed annuities, like all annuities, are tax-deferred. MYGA interest is not taxable until you withdraw the funds, at which point it is treated as ordinary income. Thus, it would be possible to roll your five-year MYGA at the end of its term into another MYGA with a higher interest rate without paying any taxes whatsoever on the gains from the MYGA and continuing to maintain the tax-deferral advantage.

2. Fixed Index Annuity (FIA)

Investors who want to do better than the fixed rates offered by a MYGA or CD will turn to Fixed Index Annuities. While growth is not guaranteed in an FIA, FIAs usually offer higher growth potential and have, over the years, proven themselves to do just that. Additionally, as with all Fixed Annuities, any gains that are earned in an FIA will never be lost when the market declines.

To illustrate the difference between FIA growth potential and CDs for example, here is Bankrate.com's list of 10-year CD rates from December 2018:

Top nationally available 10-year CDs		
INSTITUTION	APY	MINIMUM DEPOSIT
Apple Federal Credit Union	3.15%	$2,500
Discover Bank	3.10%	$2,500
Legacy Texas Bank	2.75%	$1,000
MySavingsDirect	1.65%	$1,000
Emigrant Direct	1.5%	$1,000

In comparison, as of the same date, you could purchase 10-year Fixed Index Annuities with annual caps from 6.15% to as high as 8.5%, or even some with uncapped strategies, a feature we will cover in "Discover 6 • Crediting Strategies." In most cases, an FIA should offer higher potential than CD rates (and MYGA rates as well).

The difference, of course, is that the CD or MYGA rate is guaranteed, ensuring that the specified interest rate will be paid to you no matter what happens to stocks or interest rates during the 10-year period.

While the FIA has higher potential, the interest credited to your account will fluctuate between earning nothing when the market declines and a higher rate when the market rises and interest is credited to your account. If your objective is Growth Without Risk and you decide to purchase an annuity, you will be able to rest easy knowing that principal will not be lost.

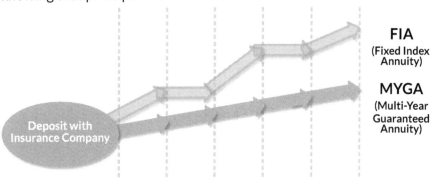

FIA
(Fixed Index Annuity)

MYGA
(Multi-Year Guaranteed Annuity)

Deposit with Insurance Company

Comparison of Guaranteed vs. Non-Guaranteed Annuity Growth Rates

In the above illustration, even though the FIA has years with zero interest credits where the market declined, the FIA is still expected to outperform the MYGA because it can capture higher gains as the market rises. Growth Without Risk investors will choose either an FIA exclusively, or combine an FIA and an MYGA, adding the MYGA to ensure that a portion of their assets gain interest every year.

3. Growth-Focused FIAs

While all Fixed Index Annuities earn interest as the market rises, there is a class of FIAs that is designed specifically for growth. Products in this class have higher caps and earning potential, but as with all products, there is a trade-off.

With a Growth Annuity, higher growth potential comes at the expense of having fewer optional benefits such as Income Riders, penalty-free withdrawals, or enhanced payouts that can offset long-term or home healthcare expenses. However, if your focus is Growth Without Risk, you are likely focused on getting the maximum return without losing principal, and you will probably be willing to forego many of these other options so you can fulfill your growth goal.

Each Fixed Index Annuity offers a different set of Crediting Strategies, the mathematical formulas which determine how your money grows, and the different indices to which they are linked. For example, you may find a Growth Annuity which is linked to the S&P 500 while others may be linked to a Pimco, BlackRock, or Bloomberg Index, and yet others to the NASDAQ or a Bond index. Most annuities will offer a variety of indexing strategies within the same contract, giving you multiple choices for growing your money.

When you delve into the details of the different crediting formulas, linked indices, and options, things can get confusing. As a result, many annuity owners leave the choice of Crediting Strategy or strategies to a financial professional much as they do the management of their investment portfolios.

Again, we'll take a closer look at Crediting Strategies in Chapter 6.

Meanwhile, the major takeaway from this chapter is that an FIA, regardless of the index and Crediting Strategy, offers the potential to outperform CDs and MYGAs at a meaningful, principal-protected rate.

5

Income Without Risk

Of all the objectives in exploring the world of annuities, the objective of Income Without Risk is the most common. People with this goal want their money to grow, but at the same time want the annuity to produce guaranteed income when they retire. Only a Fixed Index Annuity with the addition of an Income Rider can meet this goal. An Income Rider is an optional add-on benefit that produces income.

In the last chapter, we looked at how money grows in a Fixed Index Annuity. If you recall your money is linked to a market index like the S&P 500 via a mathematical formula called a Crediting Strategy. When the market and the corresponding index rise, your account earns interest—usually up to a cap specified in the Crediting Strategy you have chosen. When the index falls, nothing is lost.

This is great, but what if you want more than growth? What if you want reliable, secure, and guaranteed lifetime income without risk?

Then you will want to look at an FIA with an Income Rider.

Income Riders, often called Guaranteed Withdrawal Income Benefits (GWIB) or Lifetime Income Benefit Riders (LIBR), can satisfy this income without risk goal usually for an additional fee. It is important to remember that while an active Income Rider will generate income from an annuity, it is different from receiving an income by "annuitizing" the annuity, which we explored earlier. If you recall, when you annuitize an annuity, your principal passes to the insurance carrier in exchange for a lifetime of payments. In these cases, you lose control of your principal as it is converted into an income stream.

However, when an Income Rider is employed to produce income, the annuity's assets remain in your control rather than the insurance company's. Income payments are considered withdrawals from the cash value of the annuity. The remaining balance stays in the annuity, hopefully, to grow back and replace the amount withdrawn.

Even if the withdrawals whittle the cash value down to zero, income will continue for life. In other words, using an Income Rider allows you to get income for life but allows you to stay in control of your money.

In the illustration below, the income rider is added onto the base Fixed Index Annuity. In many annuities, the value created by the

FIA with Income Rider has two values, based on the Initial Deposit

Initial FIA Deposit

FIA Value #2 Income Value — Bookkeeping value used to determine lifetime income.

FIA Value #1 Accumulation or Cash Value — Value of the annuity in real dollars

Income Rider is a "bookkeeping" or ledger value based on the original deposit into the FIA. It is this ledger value that will determine the amount of lifetime income the annuity will provide. Think of it this way: when you purchase an annuity with an Income Rider, in most cases your original deposit creates two values—an Accumulation Value and an Income Value. The Accumulation Value is the cash or account value, while the Income Value is a bookkeeping value.

Both the Income Value and the Accumulation Value grow over time. In many instances, the income value grows at a higher rate than the Accumulation Value. The illustration below shows an FIA with an Income Rider. This Income Rider "rolls up" each year at a guaranteed interest rate of 6% (some Income Rider roll-up rates are as high as 7.5%), regardless of the rate of growth associated with the base FIA's Accumulation Value.

Income Rider With Roll-Up Rate Added to FIA
(hypothetical illustration)

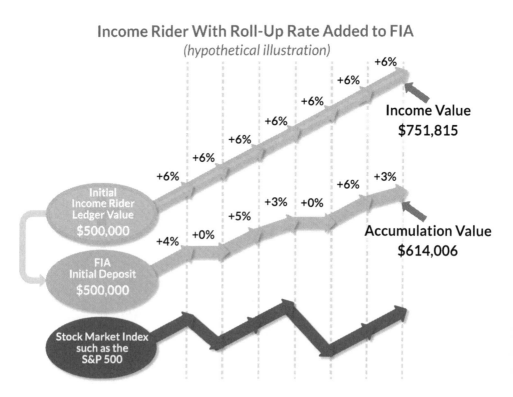

The term 'roll-up rate' is the guaranteed rate at which the Income Value of the annuity grows each year during the deferral period. So, in our example the roll-up rate is 6%. That means when the market falls, the income value will still rise at the guaranteed roll-up rate of 6% even though zero interest was credited to the Accumulation Value. Remember: roll-up rates will differ among annuities.

Eventually, after a certain period of deferring your income (let's say 5 years or 10 years), you'll want to start receiving your guaranteed lifetime income payments. Let's talk about how this income payment is calculated.

Suppose you purchased this annuity and want to know how much lifetime income the annuity will pay via the Income Rider. To find out, there is a simple calculation:

Income Rider Ledger Value   Aged-based Payout Factor   Level or Increasing Income for Life

An age-based income payout factor is a number provided by the insurance carrier that rises with the age in which you turn on the initial income payment. Let's say the payout factor for a person at age 65 is 5.0%. Here's the calculation determining their lifetime income from the illustration above :

Income Rider Ledger Value   Aged-based Payout Factor   Level or Increasing Income for Life

Based on these calculations, you could elect to receive $37,590 a year from this annuity via the Income Rider for the rest of your life.

You may elect to receive these funds monthly, directly deposited into your checking account, much like a pension or Social Security.

FIA with Level Income Rider

$500,000 Deferred Level Income Annuity

Income Deferral Period	Lifetime Income Payout Period
During which time the Income Ledger Account Value grows to $751, 815	During which time you will receive Annual Lifetime Income of $37,590

In this example we are calculating income based on a "single life payout." This means that if you passed away during the Income Payout Period, income for your spouse would end and he or she would receive the balance remaining in the annuity, usually as a lump-sum.

If you preferred that income continue for your spouse after your death, you would elect a "joint-life payout." When you select a joint-life payout, the age-based income payout factor is adjusted lower. Let's say that the joint payout factor for this annuity example is 4.5%. The joint payout would then be $33,831 annually

Level Income vs. Increasing Income

When you elect to receive income from an Income Rider you will have the choice between two types of income—Level or Increasing—depending on the type of annuity you purchase. Not all annuities and Income Riders have increasing income options available.

The income received from the Income Rider in the above examples is flat or level income; it does not rise over time to offset inflation. More current annuities offer Income Riders that can increase your income over time. These are known as rising or increasing Income Riders. They are a little more complex, but once understood, they are very compelling.

Like all riders, the increasing Income Rider is added to the base FIA contract, but not all increasing Income Riders work the same way. We've chosen a popular increasing Income Rider to use as an example so that you can get an idea of how one works and what you need to consider when making your Income Rider decision.

Unlike the level Income Rider we discussed earlier, the increasing Income Rider does not typically have a guaranteed roll-up rate. Instead, this rider's growth is dependent on the amount of interest credited to the base annuity's Accumulation Value during the deferral period.

In this example, when the Accumulation Value is credited with interest, the Income Rider value is credited with 150% of the earned interest rate. In other words, the Income Rider value earns the interest credited to the Accumulation Value plus a 50% bonus.

For instance, if the Accumulation Value has an interest credit of 4%, the Income Rider value will grow by 6% (150% x 4% = 6%). Likewise, when the market declines and no interest is credited to the Accumulation Account, the Income Rider value also receives no interest credit. Here's what that looks like:

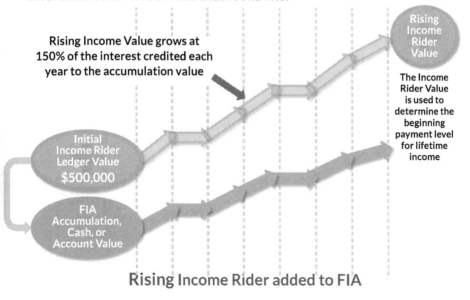

Rising Income Value grows at 150% of the interest credited each year to the accumulation value

Rising Income Rider Value

The Income Rider Value is used to determine the beginning payment level for lifetime income

Initial Income Rider Ledger Value $500,000

FIA Accumulation, Cash, or Account Value

Rising Income Rider added to FIA

Let's say you want to begin taking lifetime income. Initially, that amount is determined the same way as all other Income Riders—by taking the Income Rider value and multiplying it by a payout factor. The result is the guaranteed income the annuity will pay you each year during your lifetime.

For the sake of simplicity, let's say that at the time you want to begin income this Income Rider value is the same value as in our previous example: $751,815. Therefore, the beginning lifetime income payment rate is the same—$37,590 annually or $3,133 per month, guaranteed for a lifetime.

Beginning Lifetime Income Payment for Rising Income Rider

Income Rider Ledger Value	Aged-based Payout Factor	Level or Increasing Income for Life

Now, this is where it gets a little complicated. Remember, this is an increasing Income Rider. That means that once you start taking income payments, your income has the potential to increase each year. Let's see how.

In the product we're illustrating here, the amount of your annual income payment will increase by 150% of the interest credited to the Accumulation Value. For example: You are in the Year 1 of receiving income and receive $37,590. During that year the market index rises and the Accumulation Value of the annuity is credited with 8%. Next year, your income will increase by 150% x 8% = 12% and you will receive $42,100 in year 2.

Once your income increases to this new, higher annual payment, this payment amount is then locked in for life and can never be lowered or reduced. However, it can be increased! This process will repeat every year on your annuity policy anniversary date. In any year where interest is credited to the Accumulation Value, your income payment will rise again.

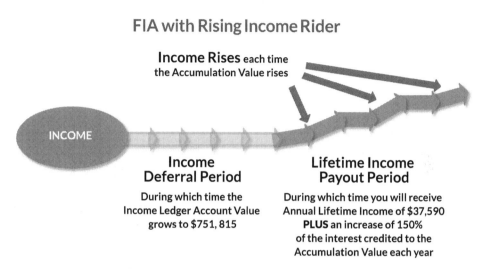

FIA with Rising Income Rider

Income Rises each time the Accumulation Value rises

INCOME

Income Deferral Period

During which time the Income Ledger Account Value grows to $751, 815

Lifetime Income Payout Period

During which time you will receive Annual Lifetime Income of $37,590 **PLUS** an increase of 150% of the interest credited to the Accumulation Value each year

What Happens When Funds are Withdrawn from an Annuity or When I Receive Income Payments?

When funds are withdrawn from an annuity as income or otherwise, that amount is deducted from the Accumulation Value. In our example, the first year of income is $37,590, so $37,590 is deducted from the Accumulation Value at that time.

The remaining amount will continue to grow based on the growth of the market, earning interest when the market rises, losing nothing when the market declines. The growth of the Accumulation Value may replenish the amount withdrawn entirely, partially, or in a down market, not at all.

A question commonly asked is what happens to your annual income payment if the Accumulation Value reaches zero? This is a fair question. After all, in any normal account (like a checking account, brokerage account, or similar), once your balance reaches zero, you can't get any more money from it. But remember, in the case of an annuity with an Income Rider, your annual income payment is guaranteed for life.

That means that even though your Accumulation Value is zero, you would continue to receive your lifetime income payments (level or rising) each and every year, for as long as you live. Upon death, however, nothing would be passed to heirs since your Accumulation Value (cash balance) is zero.

Some consider this 'free' money from the insurance company that they would have otherwise had to have taken out of their own investments. Over time, especially with the rising Income Rider, the amount of 'free' income you could receive from the insurance company can be quite substantial. This is why annuities which provide income are often called "Longevity Insurance"—they make sure that your income will always continue as long as you do.

How Does Rising Income Work? *(see diagram opposite page)*

1 During the deferral period the Accumulation Value and the Income Rider Ledger Value will grow each time the market rises and interest is credited to both accounts. When it's time to take income, the Income Rider value multiplied by the age-based income payout factor determines the beginning lifetime income payment amount.

2 Once income has begun, each time the Accumulation Value receives an interest credit, income for the following year rises by a stated percentage of the interest credit. For example, if the Accumulation Value is credited 6% in interest, income payments for the following year may increase 6%, or sometimes 6% plus a bonus amount. Once income rises to a new, higher level, that

Rising Income Illustration

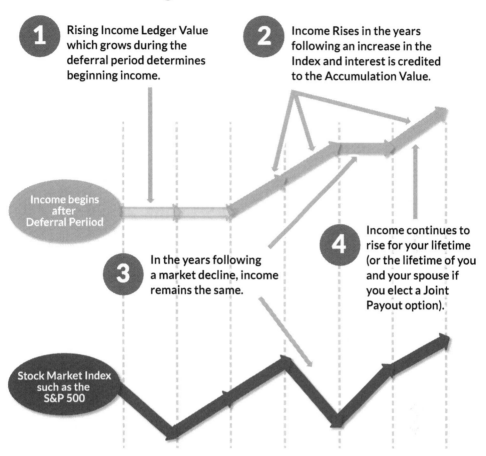

1 Rising Income Ledger Value which grows during the deferral period determines beginning income.

2 Income Rises in the years following an increase in the Index and interest is credited to the Accumulation Value.

Income begins after Deferral Periiod

3 In the years following a market decline, income remains the same.

4 Income continues to rise for your lifetime (or the lifetime of you and your spouse if you elect a Joint Payout option).

Stock Market Index such as the S&P 500

level is then guaranteed for the rest of your life (or lives if taken jointly). Income created in this type of annuity can never go down (unless you make additional withdrawals over and above the income you are receiving).

3 When the market declines and the Accumulation Value earns no interest, the income for the following year remains the same.

4 Income continues to rise for the rest of your life, or the lives of you and your spouse if you elected a joint payout option.

As you can see, Income Riders can be complex. But most have a similar concept behind them, the concept of two separate accounts— an Accumulation Value and an Income Rider Value which determines the starting amount of your lifetime income payment. Likewise, all recalculate the values within your annuity should you make additional withdrawals i.e. Penalty Free Withdrawals or withdrawals of larger amount for emergencies. But, always keep in mind that if the Account Value of your annuity should reach zero, the income always continues, and continues to rise if it's a Rising Income Rider. Once you understand these concepts you are well on your way to understanding your income options with almost any annuity you are thinking about purchasing.

How Your Money Grows:
Crediting Strategies

DISCOVER

On each 1-year Anniversary Date of your annuity purchase (the date your annuity was funded), one of the decisions you will need to make is which mathematical formula(s) you will use to determine the annual interest credited to the FIA's Accumulation Value in the coming year. These formulas are called Crediting Strategies.

Unfortunately, this part of annuities can also get confusing. There are multiple Crediting Strategies and multiple stock market indices to which they can be linked, all with their own pros and cons as well as advantages and disadvantages in various market conditions.

The S&P 500 is the most popular index to which Crediting Strategies are linked. There are many others—the NASDAQ, Russell 2000, BlackRock, Bloomberg, Pimco and more. Each has distinctive features and benefits, pros and cons. Will the index used by the FIA make a difference in performance? Yes it will, and that should be part of your decision-making process when weighing one FIA against another. Here we'll focus on a few of the more common Crediting Strategies. We will look at how they work, rather than which index they use.

Note that with most Crediting Strategies, interest is only credited to the annuity on the contract's anniversary (the date the FIA was funded, not the calendar year). Since there are no interest credits until the anniversary date, there are no value changes to review during the year.

Annual Point-to-Point Crediting Strategy

This is the simplest Crediting Strategy. The annual point-to-point strategy takes the value of the index at the beginning of the anniversary year and measures the gain (or loss) in comparison to the value at the end of the anniversary year. If there is a gain, the percentage is calculated and that year's interest is credited up to the cap. If there is a loss in the index, nothing happens and the Accumulation Value stays the same.

Point-to-Point Crediting Strategy with 5% Cap

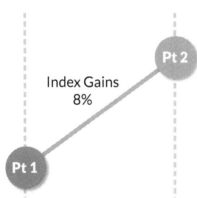

Index Gains
8%

Pt 1 – Value at the beginning of the anniversary year

PT 2 – Value at the end of the anniversary year

The index rises over the year. Therefore interest is credited to the accumulation value of the FIA up to the point-to-point cap, e.g. if the index rose 8% and the point-to-point cap was 5%, then 5% would be credited to the accumulation value of the FIA.

The fact that only the endpoints matter can work for or against you. If there are large losses during the anniversary year which are then recouped and surpassed by the end of the year, then the point-to-point strategy will be favorable (see Example B below). On the other hand, if the index rises substantially only to drop back to a lower level, then the point-to-point strategy is working against you (see Example A). For this reason, some people prefer an Averaging Crediting Strategy.

Point-to-Point Crediting Strategy in Rising and Falling Markets

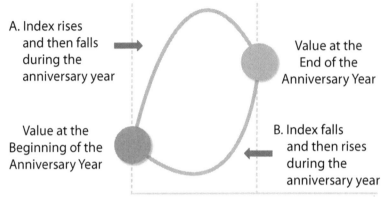

A. Index rises and then falls during the anniversary year

Value at the End of the Anniversary Year

Value at the Beginning of the Anniversary Year

B. Index falls and then rises during the anniversary year

Averaging Crediting Strategy

The averaging crediting strategy breaks the anniversary year into 12 months and averages the value of the index over that period. It then compares the average of the year with the anniversary year's starting value. Again, if there is an interest gain, that amount will be credited to the accumulation value up to the cap.

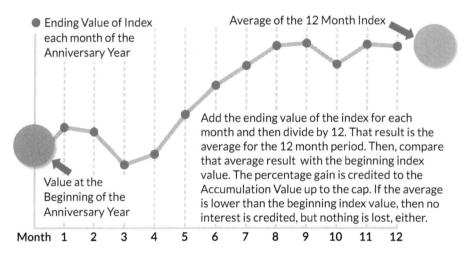

● Ending Value of Index each month of the Anniversary Year

Average of the 12 Month Index

Value at the Beginning of the Anniversary Year

Add the ending value of the index for each month and then divide by 12. That result is the average for the 12 month period. Then, compare that average result with the beginning index value. The percentage gain is credited to the Accumulation Value up to the cap. If the average is lower than the beginning index value, then no interest is credited, but nothing is lost, either.

Month   1   2   3   4   5   6   7   8   9   10   11   12

With the averaging strategy, the index's volatility is smoothed out. This cushions the results when the index falls during some months, but also limits gains when compared to the annual point-to-point strategy we explored earlier.

Monthly Point-to-Point or Monthly Sum Crediting Strategy with 2% Monthly Cap

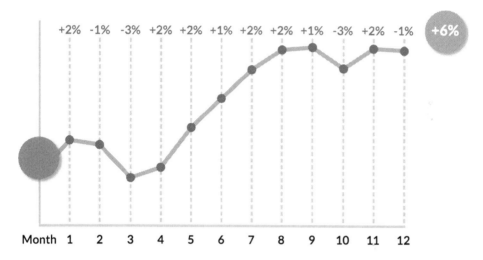

This Crediting Strategy usually has the biggest upside potential. It works especially well in steadily rising markets, but can have draw-backs in volatile markets. In this example with a 2% monthly cap, this approach offers the opportunity for annual gains as high as 24%. Monthly caps in annuity world today can range from 1% to higher than 2%. To gain 24% the market would have to rise every month above the monthly cap for one year. It's an unlikely scenario, but 24% is where this strategy would theoretically cap out. However, in more volatile markets, the monthly point-to-point strategy could yield zero gains while the annual averaging and annual point-to-point strategies might yield positive gains. Let's see why.

When calculating annual interest gains in the monthly point-to-point strategy, plus months and minus months are handled differently as follows:

1. If the index rises during a month, that percentage is included in the calculation but only up to the monthly cap. In the illustration above, the cap is 2%. So, in Month 1, if the index rises +3%, then 2%, the monthly cap, is used in the interest credit calculation. In Month 2, let's say the Index falls -1%. When the market falls the entire loss is included for that month, in this month -1%. In Month 3, the index falls -3%. So the entire -3% is applied for this month. In Month 4 the market is up +3% so that month caps out at +2%. The entire year is calculated month by month this way.

2. To determine the interest credit for the year, simply add all 12 month values together, both plus and minus (remember, plus values cannot be greater than the monthly cap). The resulting amount is the interest that will be added to the accumulation account. In this case, the annuity owner would earn +6% for the anniversary year.

3. Finally, if the sum of all monthly values is negative, zero interest is credited for the year since nothing can be lost in an FIA due to market declines.

Uncapped Strategy with Spread or Participation Rate

An uncapped strategy places no limit on the amount of interest that will be credited to the Fixed Index Annuity. It does, however, have a spread, a numerical deduction from the interest gain prior to crediting. In the following illustration, the spread is 2.5%. This means that if the index rises 8% during the anniversary year, 2.5% will be deducted and only 5.5% will be credited. Since this is an uncapped strategy, that spread remains the same no matter how much the index rises. Your interest will never cap out. Thus, if the index rises 14%, your Accumulation Value will gain a 11.5% credit because 14% – 2.5% = 11.5%.

Uncapped Crediting Strategy with 2.5% Spread

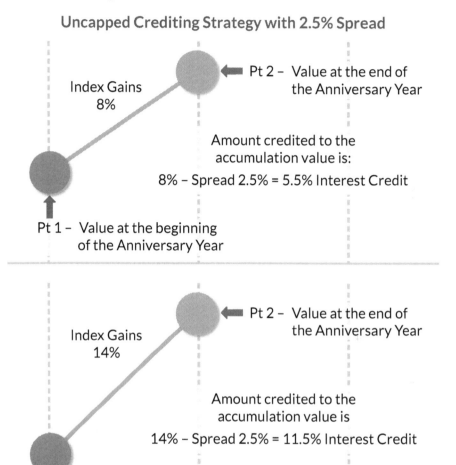

Index Gains
8%

Pt 2 – Value at the end of
the Anniversary Year

Amount credited to the
accumulation value is:

8% – Spread 2.5% = 5.5% Interest Credit

Pt 1 – Value at the beginning
of the Anniversary Year

Index Gains
14%

Pt 2 – Value at the end of
the Anniversary Year

Amount credited to the
accumulation value is

14% – Spread 2.5% = 11.5% Interest Credit

Pt 1 – Value at the beginning
of the Anniversary Year

As with all Crediting Strategies, the uncapped strategy has its own set of benefits and drawbacks. The major benefit, of course, is that the strategy is uncapped and only the spread is lost. In years where the index has big gains (assuming the spread is reasonable), FIAs can earn large interest gains. On the other hand, if the index experiences a small gain that is equal to or below the spread, the FIA will receive zero interest. While this type of uncapped strategy sounds like you can make a killing, markets and indices don't often see big, double-digit gains. Losing the smaller gains to the spread may ultimately outweigh the benefits of an uncapped strategy.

An alternate uncapped strategy employs a participation rate instead of a spread. A participation rate is a percentage of the index gain that determines the amount to be credited. Let's say you own an annuity with a 40% participation rate and the linked index rises 14%. To calculate the interest credit for your FIA, you would multiply the 14% index growth by the 40% participation rate, yielding a 5.6% interest credit.

Uncapped Crediting Strategy with 40% Participation Rate

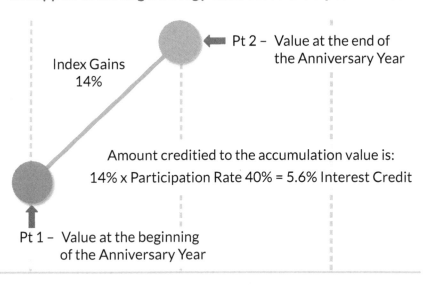

Index Gains
14%

Pt 2 – Value at the end of
the Anniversary Year

Amount creditied to the accumulation value is:
14% x Participation Rate 40% = 5.6% Interest Credit

Pt 1 – Value at the beginning
of the Anniversary Year

The world of Fixed Index Annuities offers a variety of Crediting Strategies, options, and designs. Although each strategy works differently the concept behind all strategies are the same – when the market and corresponding index rise, interest is earned; when the market and corresponding index fall, nothing is lost.

Choosing Which Crediting Strategy to Use

Each Crediting Strategy has its pros and cons and each works differently under different market conditions. If we could predict market growth and volatility, we would then be able to choose the best strategy for the upcoming year. But we can't. You might get it right here and there but over the long run trying to predict the market has been proven to be a losing proposition. Therefore, depending on the Crediting Strategies available, consider using a combination of Strategies instead of just one. For example, you might choose to allocate over three strategies:

- 25% Annual Point to Point Strategy with Cap
- 50% Uncapped Strategy with Participation Rate
- 25% Monthly Point-to-Point Strategy with Cap

Diversifying Crediting Strategies is much like diversifying your investments in the stock market. When funds are invested in the market, we know that what is a winning asset class or stock today will probably turn into a loser in the future. Likewise, what is a losing asset class or stock today will probably become a winner in the future. When you can't predict winners and losers in the market, diversification rules. The same is true for Crediting Strategies, where one Crediting Strategy may perform better in one year and not so well in another. So diversification of Crediting Strategies, we believe, is the better choice.

The Fixed Rate Crediting Option

Here's another possibility. Annuities, in addition to Crediting Strategies linked to a market index, also offer a fixed rate option which provides a guaranteed interest rate for the year, much like a CD. Typically, the fixed rate option will be lower than a one-year CD rate and should therefore be used judiciously. Often you are better off using the index-linked strategies which have much higher growth potential, even though some years you may have zero interest credited (when the market declines). The up years should offset the zero years so that you still average a reasonable return. If, however, you have allocated funds to the fixed rate strategy, you will lose the growth potential that you would have otherwise had in the index-linked strategies.

Dealing with Crediting Strategy Options and Changes

Keep in mind that each FIA will have a specific set of Crediting Strategy options available to it. So, you may find that some of the options that we've reviewed may not be offered in the FIA you are considering purchasing. Also keep in mind that the insurance carrier can, on each anniversary of the annuity, raise or lower Crediting Strategy caps, spreads, and participation rates. Those changes may also impact your selection of Crediting Strategies for the upcoming year.

For example, let's say the Annual Point-to-Point cap on an annuity is lowered from 5% to 4% for the following year, but the insurance company leaves the Annual Point-to-Point Averaging strategy the same, at 6%. Therefore, it's wise to review your Crediting Strategies annually.

Because the insurance company has the right to lower caps, spreads, and participation rates on the anniversary of the annuity, many people worry that it would be in the insurance company's self-interest to dramatically lower these rates to a minimum just after you purchased the annuity. For example, an Annuity Contract may read that the current annual point-to-point Crediting Strategy has a cap of 4%, but the insurance company can lower it as low as 1% if it so chooses. Investors often fear that they will purchase the FIA only for the insurance company to lower the cap because the company knows you would have a substantial cost from surrender charges if you bailed out of the annuity. While this is a contractual possibility, it rarely, if ever happens and is highly unlikely for the following reasons:

- Caps, spreads, and participation rates are determined by long-term interest rates as well as the cost of institutional call options for the crediting strategy in question, not an arbitrary and devious profit play by the insurance carrier.

- Movements in caps, spreads, and participation rates—up or down—tend to be similar across all insurance carriers and the FIAs they offer. If one insurance carrier decided to arbitrarily move caps to exceptionally low levels, that carrier's competitiveness and reputation would suffer. Its annuity sales would nosedive as advisors and insurance agents lost confidence in using its products for their clients.

- If you ever find yourself in the position of owning an FIA with caps that are far below the competition's, in most cases you should absorb the surrender fee and move to another product. Keep in mind that insurance companies make their profits by retaining large blocks of money, investing it long-term, and earning a small spread—the interest they earn minus their expenses and interest payments to the consumer. For carriers, frequent large outflows of funds are a sure way to bankruptcy.

On each anniversary the annuity owner receives a summary of the interest earned from each Crediting Strategy (interest is determined on the anniversary date only) and upcoming Crediting Strategy changes. All changes in allocations must be made at that time; they can never be made during the anniversary year, only on the anniversary date. This is the time to meet with the financial professional who provided you with the annuity so you can clarify your options and get input regarding potential changes. Mark your calendar!

SECTION 2

DISCUSS

Now that you have a good understanding
of the inner workings of annuities, let's take
a look at some other criteria that will be important
in helping you make your final decision about
whether to purchase an annuity.

In this section we have tried to address frequent
questions that have come up during our discussions
with prospective annuity buyers.

Remember, there are lots of opinions in the media,
advertisement, on TV and in Google research,
some of which are accurate and some not.

The *Discuss* section will help you separate
the truth from the false and give you
a much sounder understanding from which
you can make a more informed decision.

1

Annuity Liquidity

No matter your Unique Annuity Mindset, at some point the question of liquidity—your ability to access funds quickly to pay for emergency costs, repairs, and other financial demands that arise during your retirement journey—will come up. Fortunately, most investments are liquid, meaning that you can withdraw your money when you want it. But that liquidity may come with a price. That price may be determined ahead of time through a schedule, or the price will be variable, determined at the time of the withdrawal.

In market-based products, for example, liquidity costs are variable and will rise and fall depending on market conditions. When securities are sold to produce liquid funds and investments are higher in value, the cost of liquidity is zero. However, when the markets fall and investment values are down, selling securities to produce liquid assets means selling at a loss. That loss is the "liquidity cost" of market-based products and it has no limit.

If, for example, you needed cash during the 2008 market crash and had to sell when the market was bottoming out, your liquidity cost would have been huge. Let's say you had a $100,000 balance and you lost -35% during a crash, right at the time in which you needed to liquidate this account. In this scenario, a full liquidation would cost you 35%, or $35,000 to access your money. Not only would you have sustained losses on the investments you sold, but when the market rebounds, you would have owned fewer assets and been less able to take advantage of future gains.

Immediate or scheduled liquidity costs exist mostly in non-market products — cash, money markets, savings, and, of course, annuities. These costs are determined at the time of purchase so you know ahead of time what your liquidity cost will be if you decide to withdraw or liquidate your funds.

Different products have different liquidity costs and differing amounts of time it takes for you to receive your funds. Liquidating a CD prior to the end of its term typically costs six months' worth of interest (some banks may add additional penalty fees) and you would receive your funds within twenty-four hours. Taking money out of a savings account has little or no cost and your funds are available almost immediately.

Annuities are unique in that their liquidity cost is specified ahead of time for each year of the contract, usually starting at a higher percentage and going down to zero over the term of the contract. The cost of liquidity for annuities are called Surrender Charges (see diagram below).

Example 10 Year FIA Surrender Charges for Withdrawals above the Annual Penalty Free Withdrawal Limit									
Year 1	Year 2	Year 3	Year 4	Year 5	Year 6	Year 7	Year 8	Year 9	Year 10
10%	9%	8%	7%	6%	5%	4%	3%	2%	1%

So, if you need to fully liquidate your annuity, your liquidity cost would be the surrender charge that corresponds with the year of the contract that you're in. For example, if you had a $100,000 annuity balance and you needed to fully liquidate the annuity in year 6, using the table above, your liquidity cost would be 5% or$5,000.

Alternatively, another option for managing liquidity within an annuity is to purchase an annuity with a shorter surrender schedule. For example, you could purchase a 5-year annuity instead of a 10-year annuity. This would ensure that your money would be completely liquid (without surrender charges) within 5 years instead of 10.

Example 5 Year FIA Surrender Charges for Withdrawals above the Annual Penalty Free Withdrawal Limit				
Year 1	Year 2	Year 3	Year 4	Year 5
5%	4%	3%	2%	1%

Recognizing that life is full of surprises that may require immediate access to funds, many FIAs have added additional liquidity benefits for different situations. For example, let's say you only need a smaller portion of your money from the annuity, not the entire amount. Most all annuities allow for an annual 5% or 10% Penalty Free Withdrawal (usually based on your Account Value). That means you may take the specified amount at any time during the year if you find yourself in need of some extra funds.

Other annuities offer liquidity for specific situations such as the need for home healthcare, long-term care, or terminal illness, where you might be permitted to withdraw all of your funds without penalty if you find yourself in these circumstances. And others may provide what are called Income Accelerators. So, for example, if you are in Assisted Living, and are receiving income from your annuity, you may qualify to receive double or triple the amount of income during your Assisted Living stay.

The traditional knock against annuities is that your money is illiquid—that it is locked up and inaccessible if you need it. That myth is often hyped by advisors who don't use Fixed Annuities in their planning. It is also reinforced by misleading Google results and the talking points of various financial pundits who are trying to sell or promote their favorite products. Of course, when buying any financial product, you need to consider its liquidity costs and options. However, when it comes to annuities, liquidity is only 5 – 10 business days away—albeit, sometimes at a predetermined, and thus predictable, cost.

Annuity Fees

You've been around long enough to understand that when it comes to money and your finances, there's no free lunch! As an investor, you've already been conditioned to ask about fees because you know that unreasonably high fees can have a substantial negative impact on your portfolio's growth.

Over the years, you've learned that there are two types of fees— the ones you know about and the ones you discover, usually after they've claimed a sizable chunk of your earnings. The idea perpetuated by the anti-annuity crowd is that annuities are laden with high, often hidden fees. While that might be true for some annuities, it isn't the case with Fixed Index Annuities. In fact, the overwhelming majority of high-fee annuities are Variable Annuities.

However, when you read negative reviews about high annuity fees, it is uncommon for the reviewer to explain the difference between Fixed and Variable Annuities when discussing annuity fees. Most incorrectly lump both annuity types under the same high-fee umbrella, continuing to spread false and misleading information.

Unfortunately, few investors know the total fees associated with their investments. When it comes to Variable Annuities, that number is even lower. If this is you, call the insurance company from which you purchased the Variable Annuity and ask them about each of the fees listed below. Typically, the total fees will range between 3.5 – 4.5%. The expense of Variable Annuities, along with the availability of superior and less expensive Fixed Annuities, is one of the reasons for the major decline in Variable Annuity sales in recent years.

Variable Annuity Expense Description	Hypothetical	Annual Cost
Mortality & Expense Risk	1.35%[1]	($1,350)
Administrative Fees	0.25%	($250)
Optional Guraranteed Minimum Death Benefit Rider	0.61%[1]	($610)
Optional Guraranteed Lifetime Withdrawal Benefit Rider	1.03%[1]	($1,030)
Fund Expense for Underlying Funds in Variable Annuity	0.94%[1]	($940)
Total Cost	**4.18%**	**($4,180)**

[1] Source: Insured Retirement Institute, 2011 IRI Fact Book (Washington, DC; IRI, 2011), 36 – 38, 56

How onerous can these fees be? Here's an example based on one of our clients, Jim. Nine years ago, Jim invested $700,000 in Variable Annuities. He believed he was paying was about 1% in total fees. When we called the insurance carrier and asked how much the fees were, the carrier told us it was just 1%. If we hadn't asked about all the other fees on our fee hitlist, the carrier would have left it at that and Jim would have continued to believe that his fee was 1%.

After going through the fee hitlist however, it turned out the total fees were 3.41% per year. When we did the math for 3.41% of $700,000 over a period of 9 years, we found that Jim had paid $214,830 for his Variable Annuity—far greater than he thought! And that didn't even include the additional fees that would have been paid as the annuity grew in value. The question then was simple—was Jim's Variable Annuity worth it? The answer was a resounding no.

Variable Annuities are invested in the market via mutual fund like sub-accounts. There is a limited selection. If Jim wanted to invest his funds in the market, he could have done so at a far lower cost and with all the choices he wanted. And not only that, Jim could have gotten the same annuity benefits (e.g. an Income Rider) using a Fixed Annuity which would have had far lower fees, if it had any fees at all.

Fixed Index and Multi-Year Guaranteed Annuities typically have no annual fees deducted from their account values unless an Income Rider is added. If there is an annual fee for an Income Rider, it will commonly be between .9% - 1.3%. We recommend you always search for products with no fees first and see if any of them fit your planning goals. If they don't, or you find a superior Income Rider option, paying the fee may be worth it. If there is a fee, it will be calculated in one of two ways:

1. As a percentage of the Account/Accumulation Value each year.
2. As a percentage of the Income Rider Value each year.

In either case, the fee is almost always deducted from the Accumulation Value, not the Income Rider Value. While fees are deducted from your Accumulation Value, remember, your income payments will continue for as long as you live, even if your Accumulation Value reaches zero. As a result, the fee has a smaller effect on your future total income than you may think. Look at fees carefully to see how they are calculated. Remember, because of bonuses or guaranteed roll-up rates, the Income Rider Value of a Fixed Index Annuity is usually much greater than the account value. Therefore, fees calculated from the Income Rider Value will have a greater impact on your Accumulation Value than if those same fees had been calculated using the Accumulation Value itself.

When shopping around for annuities always make sure you understand the entire fee structure of the annuity, those that are apparent, and those that may be hidden deeper in the annuity's structure. There is nothing inherently wrong with paying a fee if, and only if, you get good value for the fee your paying and you can't get the same value at a lower fee. While fees aren't always the determining factor of why or why not a specific annuity is good choice, they certainly are near the top of the list and something you should focus on when evaluating your options.

Annuity Commissions

When you purchase an annuity, the person providing it must be a licensed insurance agent. Unlike Investment Advisors, who typically charge a fee for money they manage, insurance agents receive commissions on the products they sell. You do not pay these commissions; rather, the insurance company pays the agent or their employer directly.

Commission vary depending on what type of annuity it is, how long the Annuity Contract is for (i.e. 5 years vs. 10 years), and a variety of other factors, and typically range from 1% – 7%. The agent receives the commission as a lump-sum payment, a payout over the life of the annuity, or a combination of both. For example, you deposit $200,000 into an FIA that carries a 6% commission. The insurance agent will, if he or she takes the lump-sum option, receive a $12,000 commission. On the other hand, the agent may choose to receive 1% per year for the life of the annuity instead or take a 3% up front commission plus .5% for the life of the annuity. From your perspective it is irrelevant which option the agent chooses.

While you won't pay the commission out of pocket, you are wise enough to know that the insurance company has built the costs of the commission into their product. In other words, you may not pay the commission directly, but you will pay indirectly through the structure of the FIA. Be careful here for two reasons.

First, the advisor may recommend a specific product because it pays a higher commission. Second, the product might pay a higher commission because it has lower caps or limitations, making it less competitive in the marketplace. Thus, it's reasonable, when comparing annuities, to ask the financial professional you're working with to disclose the commission percentage of each annuity so that you can help ensure you're not being sold a product that is worse for you and better for the agent. If any agent you're working with won't disclose the annuity commission, be sure to walk away!

Many who argue against Fixed Index Annuities claim that they are being "pushed and sold" in the market because they offer big commissions. Taken at face value this appears to be a valid argument. After all, a $1 million deposit into an FIA could earn the agent about $60,000 in commission. That's a lot of money for sure. But peer below the surface at the agent's post-sale obligations and that same $60,000 commission, while still very fair, is not as big as it initially sounds.

Let's say you purchase an FIA with a 10-year contract period. Now the agent who sold you the annuity is responsible for meeting with you at least once a year and assisting you with any questions, distributions, and Crediting Strategy selections. Note here, however, that while conscientious agents will continue to meet with you and service your annuity, it is not a mandate or obligation to do so once the annuity is in force. But, let's say you've chosen an agent who continues meeting with you, at least on each anniversary of your annuity to review performance and discuss changes. Divide that 6% commission over 10 years of responsibility and it's 0.6% a year. Moreover, let's say you keep that annuity for another 15 years because you are drawing income from it. The agent is now responsible for managing your annuity for a total of 25 years after the date of purchase. Split 6% over 25 years and the annual commission to the agent drops to 0.24% per year.

To complicate the commission picture further, those claiming that annuity agents push their products solely for the high commissions aren't necessarily examining and discussing the alternatives. Imagine, for a moment, that instead of purchasing the annuity with a 6% commission, our hypothetical client with $1 Million chooses to have it managed by a broker (who charges commissions for trades) or professionally managed by an investment advisor for 1.00% annually (a typical management fee for that level of account).

If managed by the broker selling A-shares with front-end loads, the average front-end load (commission) is around 5.75%—surprise, surprise—closely similar to the commission on the annuity—except it comes from your pocket.

If you instead chose the money manager with the 1.00% management fee, over the following 10-year period, you would likely pay between $100,000 – $175,000 in fees (depending on the growth of your $1 million investment account). Over 25 years, the amount of fees paid to a professional money manager can be a staggeringly high amount.

Either way, you can rest assured that financial professionals, insurance agents or investment advisors are all going to be compensated for their time and effort – one way or another. It's up to you to be a savvy consumer and understand how each and every different type of professional gets paid, and then do a fee and cost-comparison between any options you are considering (like annuity vs. managed money) and see which makes the most sense. But remember, it's not just about the fees, it's also about the approach that makes the most long-term sense within your financial planning goals.

Annuity
Negativity
and
Confusion

As we've touched upon, investors researching annuities find that much of the available commentary and information fails to distinguish between two wildly different types of annuity—Variable and Fixed. For example, you may read on Google that annuities are absolutely drowning in hidden fees. That critique is directed at Variable Annuities, but most reviews don't make that clear. The fact remains that Fixed Annuities have much lower fees than Variable Annuities, and in many cases, Fixed Annuities have no annual fees at all.

Another example, a widespread ad from Ken Fisher, condemns all annuities, declaring that they are always a poor choice. While everyone is entitled to their opinion, emotionally-charged and broad

painting reviews make it difficult for regular people to look at annuities objectively.

Is Fisher talking about Variable Annuities, Fixed Interest Annuities, Fixed Index Annuities, or all annuities? Broad biases toward any product, positive or negative, contribute to a blind dislike or misunderstanding of that product. When it comes to annuities, many investors are so caught up in the negative press that they eliminate these products as a possible solution to their financial needs. In other words, their Unique Annuity Mindsets have developed in a way that rejects any consideration of annuities when they might have been a worthy consideration.

Confusion about annuities, especially the difference between Variable and Fixed Annuities, doesn't end there. The features and benefits of both annuity types may look similar but work quite differently behind the curtain. Income guarantees, for example, appear similar for both Variable and Fixed annuity products, but how each pays that income may differ substantially. On the surface fees may look similar, but dig deeper and it becomes clear that Variable Annuities contain far more than Fixed Annuities. When commentary lumps Variable and Fixed Annuities together under the umbrella term "annuities," deciphering which facts apply to which type becomes a difficult, if not impossible task.

Pros and Cons

Every financial product and strategy has its own set of pros and cons. That means every financial decision you make is a trade-off. If the pros outweigh the cons for you, you move forward, and if the cons outweigh the pros, you choose a different product. Additionally, what is viewed as a pro or con can vary from individual to individual. An objective advisor or annuity agent will share with you the pros and cons of each option and help you evaluate the trade-offs.

Compounding the problem is that while many advisors claim to be objective, they are not. Their evaluation of a product is biased based on their business model, and in that light they will exaggerate the negatives of competing products to convince you to purchase whatever it is they are pushing.

The adage "buyer beware" is more appropriate than ever when it comes to meeting with financial advisors and insurance professionals. In fact, these are two opposing factions that have been battling for market share for quite a long time—advisors who want your money in the market and insurance agents who want your money in an insurance product. Each defends its turf with great skill and enthusiasm. Each presents great arguments that support whatever they want you to buy.

The unknowing consumer can easily fall victim to a biased advisor or insurance agent's point of view. What you need to remember is that there are always two sides to the story and no right or wrong products, only products that are right or wrong for you.

The newest controversy involves recent research that supports the inclusion of an annuity as part of a modern portfolio—by replacing a portion of one's bond portfolio with a Growth Annuity or by adding a sliver of a Fixed Indexed Annuity with an Income Rider for guaranteed income (and longevity insurance). Advisors on the market side of the fence argue that they can offer better benefits than the annuity and do so with greater investment flexibility. So, from their perspective, they claim there is no benefit to including an insurance product in a portfolio.

Of course, this is not completely true. Annuities are the only product that can be 100% safe from market loss and guarantee lifetime income. While you could generate a high level of income from a well-managed portfolio invested in the market, that income will not be guaranteed, nor will the portfolio be guaranteed not to lose money in the market. That's a big difference and the underlying reason an annuity slice may make sense in most portfolios.

To be a savvy consumer, your job is to cut through all the bias and noise surrounding the product you are considering and reach the objective truth. To accomplish that, we suggest you seek out authoritative research from independent research teams. Why? A simple Google search for "Fixed Index Annuities" returns a flood of advertisements and websites, all claiming to be objective as they jockey for position on the first two pages of results.

But read the fine print, especially the disclaimer at the bottom of the article or webpage, and a different story unfolds, one that begins with, "By calling us you may be offered an insurance product for sale." It's a cunning and all too common trick: on the surface, the site claims to be independent and objective, but its real goal is to try to sell you an annuity.

Or, in the case of groups like Ken Fisher, who slams annuities at every opportunity, realize that his #1 goal is to manage your money in the market. That's all his company offers. And, as we saw in the previous chapter, that's partly due to the significantly higher amount of revenue potential that exists through money management fees. Do you think that plays any role in his emphatic assertions about annuities? Of course it does.

Below is a list of impartial, academic, and well-known industry research about annuities. Some of it is quite technical and unless you are number nerds like us, you may get lost in the details. If that's you, focus on the beginning paragraph which sets out the purpose of the research, then jump to the end of the article and read the conclusion. At the end of the day, it is the conclusions that should guide you in making the right decision about annuities.

Further Reading

Babbel, David F., and Craig B. Merrill. *Investing Your Lump Sum at Retirement.* Issue brief. The Wharton School, University of Pennsylvania. August 14, 2007. https://personalfinance.byu.edu/sites/default/files/content/77 Investing Your Lump Sum at Retirement - Babbel Merrill Aug07.pdf.

Blanchett, David, and Paul Kaplan. *Alpha, Beta, and Now...Gamma.* Technical paper. August 28, 2013. https://corporate1.morningstar.com/uploadedFiles/US/AlphaBetaandNowGamma.pdf.

Financial Research Corporation. *Income Annuities Improve Portfolio Outcomes in Retirement.* Report. January 2017. http://stolly.com/wp-content/uploads/2017/01/FRC-Annuity-Whitepaper.pdf.

Millman Inc.. *Planning With Certainty: A New Strategy for Retirement Income.* March 2017.

Pfau, Wade. *"Evaluating Investments versus Insurance in Retirement."* Advisor Perspectives. June 30, 2015. https://www.advisorperspectives.com/articles/2015/06/30/evaluating-investments-versus-insurance-in-retirement.

Cannex Research, Cannex. "Guaranteed Income Across Annuity Products: Withdrawal Guarantees Compete With Income Annuites. October 2018.

Stanford Center on Longevity. "How to "Pensionize" Any IRA or 401(k) Plan" Steve Vernon, FSA Research Scholar November 2017 Updated March 2018.

Wealthvest. "Rethinking Retirement: The Role of Fixed Index Annuities in an Optimized Portfolio" June 2017.

5

DISCUSSION

Annuity Safety

One of the first questions people ask about annuities is, "Are they safe?" This is an important question. After all, you are depositing part of your life's savings with an institution that is then charged with taking care of it, in some cases for decades. When a person parts with funds of such great significance, it is only natural—and wise—to wonder what happens if the insurance company goes out of business or doesn't own up to its obligations.

In each state, insurance companies are regulated by the Division of Insurance (DOI). It's the DOI's job to set broad financial, product, and advertising standards that protect consumers. While uncommon, an insurance company will occasionally get into financial difficulty. So, what happens if the insurance company that holds your annuity does find itself in this unlikely situation?

When you purchase an annuity, you deposit money with the insurance carrier. The insurance carrier uses these funds in a variety of ways. It will set aside a portion as a reserve against future claims. The purpose of these reserve funds, the level of which is regulated by the

DOI, is to make sure the insurance company has sufficient liquidity to pay the claims of annuity holders who are withdrawing funds either in a lump sum or as annual income. Reserve funds are invested, for the most part, in investment grade long-term bonds. The insurance company counts on the interest from these bonds to pay for all its expenses. The balance of the interest remaining after all expenses are paid is the profit margin for the insurance carrier.

When an insurance company falls into financial difficulty, there are three stages it will go through:

1. **Conservation**—This is the least harsh of the three options. During this stage, the state will work with the insurance company to ensure that day-to-day operations continue uninterrupted while a permanent solution is found.
2. **Rehabilitation**—If conservation proves ineffective, the company will go into rehab and the state will take over full operations.
3. **Liquidation**—Insurance companies that reach liquidation are considered beyond repair. In this situation, the state looks for financially stable insurers to assume the insolvent company's policies, in which case all the obligations of the annuities will be met.

While it is concerning when an insurance company gets into financial trouble, given the sheer number of insurance companies in operation, this is a rare occurrence.

But what if it does happen? This is where it's important to do your due diligence before purchasing any investment or insurance product. Always check the ratings of the insurance company. The three main rating systems are:

- A.M. Best
- Standard and Poor's
- Moody's

Each rating system clearly defines how much risk an insurance company carries. We suggest you stay with companies in the "A" range. These companies have strong ratings, meaning they stand on a solid financial foundation. Be careful however, as each system uses a slightly different methodology in their calculations. There is also no guarantee that a company with the highest rating will not experience problems. Perhaps the most useful indicator is a recent change in the company's rating. A rating increase is a good sign while a decrease may signal that this company is skating on thinner ice.

The safety of Fixed Index Annuities, combined with their potential to produce much higher returns than CDs, savings accounts, and other principal-protected instruments, explains their growing popularity. At the end of 2018, Fixed Annuity sales had soared to $132 billion, a new record. At the same time, sales of Variable Annuities rose just 2%, ending a six-year downward slide (Investment NewsNet 2/20/2019).

As a popular sub-category of Fixed Annuities, Fixed Index Annuities, also had a record-breaking year in 2018, rising 27% to $69.6 billion, the eleventh consecutive year of growth (Retirement Income Journal 4/19/2019). Todd Giesing, assistant Research Director for LIMRA Secure Retirement Institute, in a 2017 interview with Insurancenewsnet.com. said, "Of all Fixed Annuities, FIAs offer investors among the most creative and innovative product designs, which has helped power the category's sales. Benefits [of FIAs] are just stronger than on the variable annuity side."

So, are annuities safe? Despite all the protections built into insurance products like annuities, the answer to the question is a matter of probability. Based on history, the probability that you might lose money in a Fixed Annuity due to product design or insurance company failure is pretty close to zero. Unfortunately, when it comes to safety, every product or investment will have some possibility of loss. Fixed Annuities rank high on the list of products which virtually eliminate that possibility.

Annuity Bonuses

Insurance companies, from time to time, offer incentives or bonuses as a way of enhancing the potential gains of an annuity and increasing sales. In the world of annuities these are often referred to as Bonus Annuities. There are several different types of bonuses which often work differently from one another. If you are considering a Bonus Annuity, take the time to understand the bonus structure and how it works under different circumstances. But always keep in mind that while a bonus might be enticing, it should not be the sole reason for purchasing an annuity. Let's take a closer look at the different types of bonuses available.

Up-Front Premium Bonus

An Up-Front Premium Bonus is a lump sum that the insurance company credits to your Accumulation or Cash Value Account which is based on the premium deposit you make when you initially purchase the annuity. For example, let's say you place $100,000 in an annuity that has a 10% Up-Front Premium Bonus. The insurance company immediately adds 10% or $10,000 to your account and when the policy is issued to you, its value will be $110,000.

Lump-Sum Income Account Bonus

If you recall, Income Annuities most often have two separate accounts —the Accumulation Value or Cash Value account and an Income Rider Value account. An Up-Front Income Rider Account Bonus is a lump-sum that the insurance company credits to your Income Account based on the premium deposited when you purchase the annuity.

For example, let's say you deposit $100,000 into an annuity. Now, your Accumulation Value is $100,000. But, let's say that the insurance company is offering a 22% Up-Front Income Account Bonus. That means that your Income Account value at the time of purchase will be $122,000. This can be a bit confusing because your deposit of $100,000 created two different accounts, one which does not get a bonus, the Accumulation or Account Value, and one which does, the Income Account Value, which some call the Protected Income Value or Lifetime Income Benefit Rider (LIBR).

Up-Front Income Account bonuses are quite valuable as it is the Income Account value which will determine your guaranteed annual lifetime income amount in the future when you decide to take income from your annuity. The higher this value, the higher your income will be at this time. Typically, the purpose of purchasing an income focused annuity is to get the highest guaranteed lifetime income possible. Up-Front Income Account bonuses help achieve this goal.

Growth Bonuses

Growth bonuses may be applied by the insurance company to either the Accumulation Account or to the Income Account. Let's say that your annuity grows by 4% and you are to receive a Growth Bonus of 50% to the Accumulation Account. In this instance, the Accumulation

Account would grow by 6%. So, if your annuity's Accumulation account was valued at $100,000 and it earned 4% then it would be worth $104,000. But then a 50% bonus is added. The value of the Accumulation account would be $106,000.

On the other hand, the bonus may be applied to the Income Account instead of the Accumulation Account. Once again, let's say the Accumulation Account grows by 4% but your annuity has a 50% Income Account Growth Bonus. Then your Income Account would grow by 6%. For example, your Accumulation Value is $100,000 and your Income Account Value is $150,000. The annuity earns 4% which is credited to your Accumulation Account which rises to $104,000. But then it adds 6% credit to your Income Account which now rises from $150,000 to $159,000. Growth bonuses on the Income Account, just as Up-Front Bonuses in the Accumulation Account all serve to boost guaranteed lifetime income when it is begun in the future. Can an annuity have both an Up-Front Income Account Bonus in addition to a Growth Bonus? Yes, it can. Bonuses come in many shapes and sizes and there's no end to their creativity.

Vesting of the Bonus

Okay, you've you purchased a Bonus Annuity with a 10-year surrender period. But, let's say you decide you need to cash in your annuity before the end of the surrender period due to an emergency. Or, suppose you die before the end of the surrender period. Do you get to keep the bonus given to you or do you have to pay all or part of them back? Well, here's the scoop. Let's take the easy one first.

If you pass away during the term of most all annuities, not only do all the surrender charges get waived, but any bonus you received is immediately vested. Vesting is the amount of the bonus that you own. On death your annuity bonus become 100% vested. This means that your heirs will receive the full amount of the bonus funds.

On the other hand, many annuity bonuses have a vesting schedule. This is a percentage of the bonus you own over time. A typical vesting schedule might be structured like this. Each year, 10% of your annuity bonus is vested. Should you draw funds from the annuity in years prior to 100% vesting, a proportional amount of the bonus will be given back to the insurance carrier. For example, let's say you decided in year 5 to cash in or surrender your annuity. This means that 50% of the bonus is vested, which you will receive. The balance of the bonus funds showing in your account will go back to the insurance company.

Bonuses and their vesting schedules can be very complex. Always remember that while a bonus sounds great, you need to spend some time understanding how that bonus is credited and vested. Otherwise, that bonus may end up back in the insurance company's pocket instead of yours.

Are Annuities Too Good to be True?

Many people wonder if Fixed Index Annuities, a product class that doesn't lose money when the market declines and earns money when the market rises, are too good to be true. Most people also understand that insurance companies are in business to make a profit and believe there must be something nefarious in an FIA that they're missing, a "gotcha" hidden in the fine print.

Surprisingly, many people don't seem to realize that it is possible—and usually preferable—for insurance carriers to offer a product that benefits both company and consumer. Let's take a closer look at how insurance companies can offer FIAs that are a win-win for you and them.

Here's the scoop: when you deposit money into an annuity, the insurance company invests the funds in long-term bonds—mostly government bonds—which earn an interest rate. Let's say the bonds earn an interest rate of 3.5%. Out of the 3.5% the insurance company receives on billions of invested dollars, it must now pay all its expenses. Let's assume those expenses add up to 2% of the 3.5% earned, leaving 1.5% to share with you. When an FIA is funded, instead of the insurance company giving you the interest rate of 1.5%, they use the equivalent amount of money to purchase institutional call options. The options create the interest gain opportunity for you to earn in your FIA.

If the market goes up, the insurance company will exercise the option and credit your account with interest. If the market falls, the insurance company loses the cost of the option and you earn nothing. So, both you and the insurance company win whether the market goes up or down.

There are still some people who feel that an annuity is a bad product because the insurance company "always makes money" and as a result, it must not be good for the consumer. Let's think about that for a moment. The truth is, yes, of course the insurance carrier makes money. The insurance company, like any business, exists to earn revenue and create a profit. If it were never to make money, then nobody would want to run that business, and it would cease to exist.

However, this is true of all businesses. Imagine, for a moment, that you go out to eat at a restaurant that you love. Is it a bad thing for that restaurant to make a profit? If, in fact, that restaurant didn't make a profit, it would cease to exist, and then you lose out on the opportunity to eat the food you enjoy.

This same concept is especially true in the stock market. In fact, in the market, every single stock is a company that is trying to maximize its profitability for its shareholders. Thus, when assessing whether to purchase something for yourself, focus on analyzing if it's a good deal for you, and avoid focusing on whether the company on the other side is making money.

Some people ask "why pay the insurance carrier to do what I can do on my own?" They think they can bypass the insurance company and can construct their own version of FIAs by using a combination of

CDs, MYGAs, Bonds, Options and other market investments. While this is theoretically possible, it's quite complex, carries greater risk, and cannot duplicate the 'longevity insurance' and income guarantees that annuities offered by insurance carriers provide.

In other words, only an annuity can provide the guarantee of lifetime income. Other methods can provide the promise of lifetime income, but not the guarantee. That's a huge difference. Any time you hear someone claim that you should never buy an annuity because they can provide a better income alternative, just ask if their alternative is 100% guaranteed for life, even if the Accumulation Value reaches zero. If they say its 100% guaranteed then ask them to sign off on that in writing. You'll find they will never sign their name to a guarantee of performance and lifetime income as the insurance carrier will.

When a product seems too good to be true you should probably run in the other direction. At first glance, this seems to describe Fixed Index Annuities. But when you look under the hood at the rationale behind their construction, their historical performance, record of reliability, and understand their purpose and where they fit into you financial plan, Fixed Index Annuities prove to make a lot of sense.

IRAs or 401(k)s in Annuities

Can you purchase an annuity with your qualified funds? You sure can, and many people do. This is called an IRA Annuity. Qualified funds are tax-deferred, often siloed in IRAs, 401(k)s, 403(b)s, and TSAs. In fact, in our experience, nearly 60% of annuity buyers make their purchase with qualified money, and this seems to be an industry norm. Since qualified IRAs and other funds are already tax-deferred, many people question the wisdom of depositing these funds into a product that touts tax-deferral as one of its main benefits. The answer to this question is three-fold.

First, if a you're the type of person who leans toward guaranteed principal, a Fixed Index Annuity, because of its growth potential, may be the product of choice. So, while an IRA inside an annuity already has the advantage of tax-deferral, individuals who purchase an annuity with qualified funds are looking to take advantage of the FIA's other benefits. As we've discussed, these benefits include, but are not limited to:

- A safe place for retirement savings

- Protection from market declines
- The opportunity for lifetime income
- A more efficient management of RMDs (Required Minimum Distributions)
- Greater tax-efficiency
- Superior growth potential in relation to other principal protected products i.e. CDs
- Low or zero fees

The second reason it may make sense to put IRA funds into an annuity has to do with the efficient management of your RMDs. When the owner of a traditional IRA turns 70 ½, he or she is mandated by law to begin taking distributions from their IRA. This is why they are called "required" distributions; you have no choice. Even if you don't need the funds from your IRA, even if the market is in the gutter and you don't want to sell shares at a depressed price, you must take your RMDs for that year (unless you want to pay a big penalty). RMDs are non-negotiable, whether you need the money or not and whether the market is up or down.

Since Required Minimum Distributions are not optional, many people elect to take them from their FIAs rather than investments in the market. Because these annuities don't lose value when the market declines, you will never be in the position of having to sell at a lower price when the market has declined and you need to take your RMDs. Selling when the market is slumping is rarely a good idea and often undermines the ability to recoup losses (there is less money in the account to grow when the market rises).

Moreover, if you are taking income from the IRA annuity, that income may not only cover the RMD for that annuity, it may be sufficiently large enough to cover the RMDs that need to be taken from other qualified accounts—other IRAs, 401ks, 403bs and TSAs. If you recall, RMDs don't have to be taken from each qualified account. They may all be taken from one account as long as the total RMD requirement is met.

Finally, IRA withdrawals are always taxable. Today, there is no way around paying taxes on RMDs or any withdrawal from an IRA for you or your heirs. On the other hand, non-qualified monies on which you've already paid the taxes may currently be passed along to heirs with a step-up in basis. That means that growth in your non-qualified accounts will have a tremendous tax advantage to your heirs when you pass. If those accounts were in an annuity, the growth over the principal deposited (interest earned) will be taxable to you and your heirs as ordinary income when withdrawn.

So, if you have the choice of including qualified money or non-qualified money in the annuity, we would lean towards the using the qualified money first. However, that absolutely does not mean that you shouldn't deposit non-qualified funds in an annuity. The bottom line is that if you want growth without risk or guaranteed income and that is your top priority, you need to use whatever funds available, qualified or non-qualified.

Consider Longevity

Somewhere in your annuity purchase decision process it would make sense, we believe, to have a clear understanding of how long you might live. In other words, your longevity.

While it's true that no-one can predict the length of their life, we can use statistics and probability to help your evaluation. After all, an annuity that creates income is longevity insurance. Whereas life insurance is designed to protect your family if you die prematurely, annuities are designed to protect your family with sufficient income if you live a long life.

The picture looks like this:

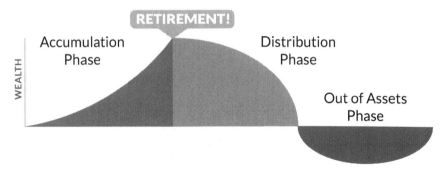

RETIREMENT!

Accumulation Phase

Distribution Phase

Out of Assets Phase

WEALTH

At first, prior to retirement, you are in the Accumulation Phase, accumulating and growing your savings. After retirement you move into the Distribution phase, using your savings for income when your paycheck stops. As long as your money lasts, things are good. But what happens if you run out of money during your retirement? What are your choices? Here are the options that are typically available if, during your retirement, you discover that you have insufficient funds to last through your distribution phase.

Options When You Run Out of Money in Retirement	
1	Lower your lifestyle and standard of living.
2	Apply for government assistance.
3	Go live with your kids.
4	Ask your family members for money.
5	Go back to work.

None of these options look too appetizing do they? With this in mind, it should be no surprise that when the question was asked to a group of people between the ages of 44 – 75 about which they feared more—running out of money or death, that 61% said that they were more afraid of running out of money than dying. The problem is that the longer you live, considering general inflation and the rising costs of healthcare and long-term nursing care, the probability of running out of money rises.

Which Do You Fear More?

Study by Allianz Life Insurance Company

So, what are your chances of living a long life? Most people underestimate how long they are going to live, so these statistics may be an eye-opener for you. The following chart illustrates the likelihood of your living to 80 or 90 years old if you are 65 today. A 65-year-old male today, has a 63% chance of living to age 80; a female has a 73% chance of living to 80. But, if you are married, there is a 90% chance that one person in the couple will live to 80.

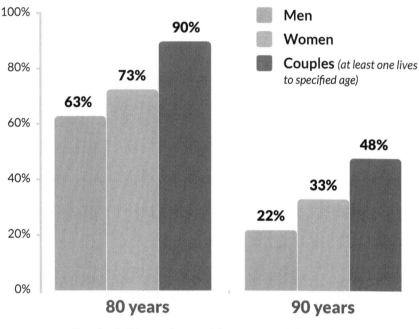

Probability of reaching ages 80 and 90

Persons aged 65, by gender, and combined couple

On the other hand, if you are 65-years-old today, a male has a 22% chance of living to 90; a female has a 33% chance of living to 90; and one person in a married couple has a 48% chance of living to 90. Take a step back and think about that, especially if you are a female or you are a married person where the probabilities of longevity are higher. Also, keep in mind that these statistics don't include how much longer you may live past 80 or 90. The oldest person in the world lived to 116. Could that be you? Many people live far longer than they think they will. Will your money last?

Longevity insurance through the use of annuities assure that your money will last and that it will not be lost during a market decline. For those seeking peace of mind about safety and income, FIAs have proven since their introduction over 20 years ago that they are a reliable source of income and growth on which you can depend and from which you can sleep well at night.

Keep longevity in mind when making your decision about annuities. While there may be specific aspects of annuities that are of concern to you, you may find that the guarantees and peace of mind that annuities provide may well outweigh these concerns.

10 Purchasing an Annuity

The first step on your way to purchasing an annuity is, of course, to make sure an annuity is the right product for you. The following section, "Decide," will help you make that decision. In this section we are going to take a look at how to purchase an annuity once you've decided to buy one.

Keep in mind, and we can't say this often enough, that your first goal is to work with an advisor or insurance agent that will provide objective information about the various annuity options. An objective agent will not try and push you towards one annuity or another but will explain the pros and cons of each annuity with regards to your goals so that you can make an informed choice.

You will probably have a number of annuity options to choose from with many similar designs, making it difficult to figure out which would be better for you. Here's where it would be a good idea to rely on your agent to help you narrow the field. Otherwise, you may find yourself overwhelmed with information and choices, so much so that you can't make a decision at all. Perhaps you've heard the phrase 'analysis paralysis'. Without some professional help in sifting through the many annuities on the market, 'analysis paralysis' may kick in and freeze you from making a decision that is quite important for your future financial wellbeing.

Once you have selected an annuity, you will need to fill out an application provided by the insurance company offering the annuity you want to purchase. Your application will then be reviewed by the insurance company to make sure it meets certain financial standards and that the product is suitable for you. If your application moves forward, then the insurance company, upon receipt of the funds you are going to deposit in the annuity, will send your contract to you or to the professional who assisted you.

The insurance carrier may accept funds in the form of a check, a transfer from another annuity (called a 1035 exchange), a transfer from another investment account, or custodial transfers of qualified money held in an IRA, 401(k), TSA, or 403(b), which would not be subject to tax.

Once you receive your contract, you will have a specified amount of time to read the contract and make sure it works exactly as you understood it. This is called a "free look" period—typically the first 15 – 30 days after the date you receive your contract in hand. If you discover anything in the contract that makes you uncomfortable or that you expected to be different and want to cancel the contract, you can do so without penalty during the free look period. All you have to do is tell the insurance company that you are "free-looking" (cancel-ing) your contract and the funds you deposited will be returned to you, usually within 10 business days.

The good news is that most insurance carriers do a great job making their contracts understandable and easy to read. Inside the contract, you will find all the details of your annuity, including the amount deposited, contract number, contract period, all fees and potential charges, selected Crediting Strategies, and all the definitions for specialized vocabulary used in the contract. While some parts will be highly detailed, in comparison to a decade ago, today's contracts are far more consumer-friendly.

Ultimately, you can feel confident that, even after completing the annuity application, you will have ample opportunity to review your new annuity contract, discuss all the details, confirm how everything works and ensure that it was the right decision for you.

Finding the Right Advisor

We believe it's essential that you work with an agent or advisor who upholds the Fiduciary standard to its highest level. The person who excels as a Fiduciary will always put your interests first, no matter what. A true Fiduciary will never try to "sell" you something or push you in one direction or another. He or she will look at all financial and insurance products objectively, explain the advantages and disadvantages of each, and help you determine which are the best choices to help you reach your goals.

Insurance agents, as professionals who are only licensed to sell insurance products, are not implicitly required to uphold a Fiduciary standard. They are many insurance agents, however, that will adhere to the Fiduciary standard even though they are not required to do so. On the other hand, professionals with the title Investment Advisor Representative (IAR), who represent a Registered Investment Advisory (RIA) firm, are required by law to meet the Fiduciary standard. When you meet with a financial professional, your first question should be: "Do you uphold a Fiduciary Standard?"

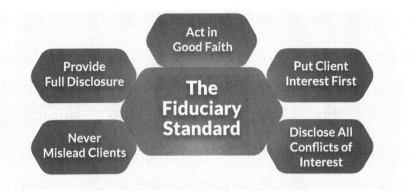

Principles of the Fiduciary Standard

According to the Securities and Exchange Commission rules and the Investment Advisors Act of 1940, the five responsibilities of a Fiduciary are:

- Put the client's interests first
- Act with the utmost good faith
- Provide full and fair disclosure of all material facts
- Don't mislead clients
- Expose all conflicts of interest

Why is this so important? Let's use an everyday example: buying a car. Assume you are looking for a car that costs less than $25,000 and gets more than 25 miles per gallon. There are probably a long list of cars that meet those requirements. So, most of us would do additional research. You might include which cars have the best safety features, which have a better maintenance or repair history, which will have a smoother ride, or the best resale value. You search to find that car that meets your basic needs but has other features that makes it the very best car for you.

Now, let's say you are in a Ford dealership. The only cars that are sold there are Fords. Would you feel comfortable that the salesperson representing Ford would find the best car—out of all available cars in the market—for you? Of course not. He may find the best Ford for you but would never tell you to go down the street and try Chevy or some other manufacturer that offers different features and benefits. If the salesperson upheld the Fiduciary Standard he would shop all the cars to find the best one for you, not just the one he represents. When it comes to selecting who you work with to purchase an annuity make sure you find the person who is independent and who is loyal to you.

Another consideration when purchasing an annuity, in addition to whether your advisor is acting as a Fiduciary, is whether they are 100% independent as an insurance agent. For example, a Captive Agent is an insurance agent who works for a big insurance company, say American General, for example. As a result, this Captive Agent may be required by his company to only promote American General products. This is a conflict of your best interests. What if a better product exists elsewhere? Unfortunately, most Captive Agents will only represent their own company's products and won't provide you with many (or any) alternative company products.

Instead, by working with an independent insurance agent, you can help ensure that you're getting better choices and flexibility. Independent agents should have the ability to provide you quotes from nearly every major insurance company that's in the marketplace. This provides you with more options to review and more likelihood to find the best annuity product possible.

One last item for consideration. Just because an Advisor is a Fiduciary, they may or may not be objective in their recommendations. Some investment advisors will negate the value of insurance products like annuities because their broker-dealer or investment advisory firm prohibits their sale, because they simply don't understand them (and haven't taken the time to), or because they earn more revenue by having your funds invested in the market.

Remember, when you meet with a financial professional, we

suggested your first question should be: "Are you a Fiduciary?" If the answer is yes, the next question should be, "Are you a Holistic Fiduciary that will potentially include annuities in your planning?" A Holistic Fiduciary is objective about all products and asset classes and will utilize both market and insurance products without bias, as long as those products are the best products for you. Holistic Fiduciaries, unfortunately, are rare birds in the financial community.

If when asking this question you hear a response such as "No, we don't like annuities" or "Oh, you should never buy annuities" then you know that you're working with a biased Fiduciary (not a true Fiduciary) and you should look elsewhere. Remember, annuities have pros and cons and may be a fit for you, so they should at the very least be reviewed and considered in your plan, and they certainly aren't all bad!

Like any other group, there are advisors and insurance agents who will look out for your best interests and there are others who are just trying to make a buck and will sell you anything they can (like the bad apples of any industry). To ensure you're getting the best advice possible, including about annuities, we recommend that you do the following steps:

- Choose a Holistic Fiduciary when possible
- Don't work with an advisor who says Annuities are bad
- Don't work with an agent who bashes the market, either
- Work with an Independent Insurance Agent/Agency
- Ensure you compare multiple insurance products
- Ask what the commissions are on different products
- Never feel rushed or pressured to make a decision
- If you're feeling uncertain or unsure, shop around

Following these steps can help you feel confident that you're getting the annuity and financial advice that is truly best for you!

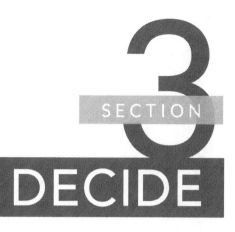

SECTION 3

DECIDE

Now that you understand how annuities work and have a more objective view of many of the important questions and opinions surrounding annuities, you are in a position where you can begin to finalize your decision about whether an annuity is right for you.

This *Decide* section focuses on a step-by-step process of identifying which of your assets might be a suitable for annuities, how much should be deposited in an annuity, and which type of annuity would best help you meet your investment goals.

While decisions about where to invest your hard earned savings are not simple nor easily made, we hope that the information and steps we provide here will serve to help you make the best decision possible, one in which the pros clearly outweigh the cons, where you are confident that you are making the right decision, and where your know that decision will give you greater peace of mind and a better night's sleep in the future.

1

Should an Annuity be Part of My Portfolio?

The simple answer is yes, as current research says that annuities should be included in your portfolio. The complex answer is maybe. Both Morningstar and other research (see page 78 for a list of research articles and papers) suggest that including a slice of an annuity in your portfolio will meaningfully enhance income and equivalent portfolio growth (called Gamma).

But while the research is clear, each person has his or her own goals, asset levels, desired income, and feelings about incorporating an annuity product in his or her portfolio. So it's not wise to include an annuity in your portfolio solely because the research suggests you should. A closer look at portfolio design will help you with your decision process

Older portfolios were primarily designed around stocks and bonds. Today, most investors still plan their investments around this stock and bond strategy, with more conservative portfolios made up of a higher percentage of bonds and more aggressive portfolios a higher percentage of equities.

In a perfect world, when stocks decline in value, bonds would rise, hedging the portfolio's overall loss. Recently, due to an extremely low interest rate environment and other political and economic factors, bonds have not behaved as reliably as in the past. This is one reason newer market-based portfolios now include alternatives—a combination of REITs, commodities, and managed futures— which act as a downside hedge for the bond side of the portfolio.

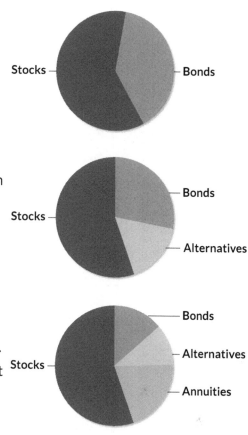

Now, as we have seen, current research suggests the inclusion of an annuity as another asset class to further diversify your portfolio, mitigate downside losses, and at the same time provide a guaranteed lifetime income. A modern portfolio includes stocks, bonds, alternatives, and an annuity in ratios based on personal goals, risk tolerance, and future needs. When the market falls and equity prices decline, the annuity portion of your portfolio will maintain its value (remember, FIAs lose nothing when the market drops) and continue to deliver income at the same rate, ensuring the market decline does not impact your standard of living.

Portfolios that include all major classes of equities, bonds, alternatives, and insurance are said to have "optimized portfolio management." Ultimately, investors who cling to their anti-annuity biases despite contrary evidence miss out on the stability and heightened performance an annuity can bring to their portfolio.

Should you add an annuity to your portfolio? At the end of the day that is a personal decision. From our perspective, we always fall back on good research when making financial decisions. A research-based approach cuts through the biases of your own emotions, "stuff" you have heard from the media, the internet, friends, and traditional advisors, and helps you make wiser, clearer decisions. The best thing you can do is work with a person you trust, run the numbers and see directly how an annuity may fit within your plan.

2 Determining Your Red & Green Money Ratio

When considering purchasing an annuity, you will need to find the appropriate ratio for allocating funds between Red (market-based products) and Green Money (principal-protected products with no market risk, like annuities). And because each of us is unique in the way we think about money and investments, each of us will make that determination differently. There are a few different methods you can use to determine how much you should allocate into annuities.

One starting point is to use an old rule of thumb called the Rule of 100. The Rule of 100 says that you should take the number 100 and

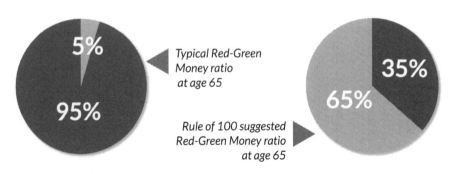

Typical Red-Green Money ratio at age 65

Rule of 100 suggested Red-Green Money ratio at age 65

subtract your age. The balance is the amount you should invest in Red Money products while the rest of your money stays safe in Green Money products.

For a 65-year-old, the Rule of 100 would look like this: 100 minus 65 equals 35. According to the Rule, you should invest 35% of your money in the market and place the remaining 65% in an FIA or other Green Money Product. The Rule is based on the thinking that as you get older you have less time to recoup market losses. Therefore, you should have more deposited in principal-guaranteed Green Money Products which are safe from loss.

Another way to look at your allocation between Red and Green Money is as two triangles, one stacked on top of the other. For ease of calculation, let's say you have $1,000,000 at age 65. The Rule of 100 suggests you portion out $650,000 as Green Money and $350,000 as Red Money. Examine the diagram below. Notice how stable the triangle is with the appropriate asset allocation? Even if you had big losses in your Red Money, your Green Money would remain un-touched, stabilizing your entire portfolio, especially when you don't have time to fully recoup losses.

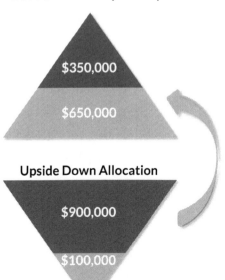

$350,000

$650,000

Upside Down Allocation

$900,000

$100,000

At 65 years old, the Rule of 100 says assets should be adjusted to 65% Green Money and 35% Red Money. Note how stable this is. Even if there are substantial market losses, the Green Money will stabilize the entire portfolio.

The rule suggest that this person, who is 65, should consider moving $550,000 into Green Money to stabilize his or her portfolio.

This person is upside-down according to the Rule of 100. There is too much instability for his or her age.

Unfortunately, many people we meet have their Red and Green Money allocations upside down. They are, in other words, taking too much risk for their age. The triangle for this allocation is top-heavy, left balancing precariously on its point, ready to topple should the market fall or turn volatile.

Remember, that the Rule of 100 is just a starting point, not a hard and fast rule. For example, you are 55, and although you have made money in the market, you are now nearing retirement and wary of a big loss. Additionally, your growth goal for your market-based portfolio is 6%. Following the Rule of 100, you consider moving funds so that your allocation is 55% Green Money and 45% Red Money, but you are still worried about losses. You could consider shifting a higher percentage to Green Money than the Rule suggests.

If you purchased a Fixed Index Annuity with your Green Money, you may not earn as much as your market goal, but you would sleep well at night, which at this time in your life may be more important to you.

On the other hand, if you were more of a risk-taker or have a substantially higher amount of assets and market-loss doesn't impact you as heavily, you might weight your allocation toward Red Money and deviate from the Rule in that way.

Use the following table to determine your anticipated growth rate when you use a combination of Red and Green investments. This rate will always be lower than the rate you might achieve if you left most of your funds in the market. If you want growth without risk, your job is to evaluate the trade-off of lower returns for greater stability in your portfolio. Unfortunately, this is another situation where you can't have your cake and eat it too.

Total Portfolio Rates of Return
Using the Rule of 100 at Various Ages

Age	% Red Money @ 6%	% Green Money @ 4%	Total Portfolio Rate of Return
50	50%	50%	5%
55	45%	55%	4.9%
60	40%	60%	4.8%
65	35%	65%	4.7%
70	30%	70%	4.6%
75	25%	75%	4.5%

As you can see from the above table, when compared to an annuity, taking significantly more risk doesn't always add a significant amount to your return. And, during periods of market volatility and loss, Green Money products can, in fact, provide the ability to outperform the market due to protecting your principal and not needing time to recover from losses.

Talk through your Red/Green Money allocation with your advisor, and together, you can work to determine the appropriate amount of each that fits best for you and your plan.

How Much Should I Put Into an Annuity?

Many people decide how much to put into an annuity by first figuring out the amount of guaranteed income they want. Let's say you spend $75,000 a year with $60,000 devoted to essential expenses such as property taxes, mortgages, healthcare expenses, insurance premiums, utilities, food, clothing, rent, gas, etc. Meanwhile, the remaining $15,000 is devoted to paying optional expenses—eating out, movies, gifts, donations, special occasions, trips, your play money, and so on.

Traditionally, most people only have only their Social Security and pension (if they have one) as their guaranteed income. The rest of their income comes from market investments, which can rise in good years and falls in bad years, reflecting the movements of the market. This can create high levels of income uncertainty and persistent anxiety about future market performance. Instead, let's say you want to cover all your essential expenses with guaranteed income from an annuity which provides more safety and security. Let's see how this might work.

1. You want your guaranteed income to pay $60,000 of expenses.

2. Currently, your guaranteed annual income consists of $35,000 from Social Security and $10,000 from your pension. This gives you a total guaranteed income of $45,000.

3. Subtract the amount of income you already receive ($45,000) from your goal ($60,000). The remaining $15,000 is the amount of guaranteed income you are short. This is the guaranteed income you will need to get from your annuity purchase.

4. Consider: how much will you need to deposit into an annuity to provide $15,000 of guaranteed income?

To answer this question, we need to go back to how guaranteed income is calculated in a fixed income annuity. If you recall, that calculation is based on a factor derived from your age. For example, in many annuities, the factor for a person at age 60 is 5%. This factor would then be used to divide the desired amount of guaranteed income, in this case, $15,000. So, $15,000 divided by 0.05 is $300,000. This is the amount you would need to deposit in an annuity with a .05% income factor.

Keep in mind that this is a very simple example. There are several other factors that need to be considered and calculated:

1. You may defer your income well into the future. If you do, then your money will have time to grow. As a result, you will need to deposit less into the annuity than if you needed income immediately.

2. Each annuity will have a different income factor (the number you use to determine the amount of income your annuity will pay). While you may shop around to find the highest income

factor, be careful as you might lose too much growth potential or other benefits by focusing solely on income.

3. You will need to decide whether you want flat or rising income (to offset inflation). Typically, annuities with rising income will begin paying income at a lower rate than a flat income annuity. Will this work for you? Is it worth the trade-off? Do you need a combination of the two?

Most people who choose to have a high percentage, if not all of their retirement income guaranteed, tell us that the prime motivation for doing so is to give them greater peace of mind. Knowing that their retirement income is guaranteed for the rest of their lives, that they will never outlive their income or find themselves in a situation where they may have to depend on others or cut back on the quality of their living, seems to give everyone greater confidence, less worry, and a sense of greater stability. And, perhaps most importantly, it provides peace of mind about their future that they could not find through any other financial strategy.

When determining how much you are going to deposit into the annuity you purchase, keep in mind that the benefits of an annuity are far greater than just the monetary numbers. At the end of the day, we believe that money is a means to an end, to give you the kind and quality of life that you want and deserve.

DECISION

Identifying Buckets of Money Suitable for Annuity Deposits

Sometimes, deciding to make a deposit into an MYGA or FIA is simply a matter of identifying a specific bucket of money that you want to keep safe while it grows at a reasonable rate. These are the buckets most people identify as potential annuity deposits:

| IRA, 401(k), 403(b), etc. Rollover | Ignored Money | CD Purchases or Coming Due | Excess Savings | Required Minimum Distributions (RMD) | Never Touch Money |

IRA, 401(k), 403(b), TSA, SEP, and Roth Rollover Buckets

If you're like most people, you've accumulated your retirement assets by making contributions to some form of retirement account such as an IRA, 401k, TSA, SEP, or Roth. These are easy buckets of money to identify and a Fixed Index Annuity may be an excellent place to deposit these funds instead of leaving them in the market. Here are typical situations in which these buckets are ear-marked for annuities:

IRA, 401(k), 403(b), etc. Rollover

- You've changed jobs, but your 401(k) is still at your old company.
- You've rolled your old 401(k) into the 401(k) set up by your new employer, but leave it there believing you can't roll it into an IRA or annuity which may be better suited to help you reach your retirement goals.
- You've just retired. You know the investment options for your 401(k), if you leave it at your old company, are limited (and perhaps expensive).

Ignored Money Buckets

Ignored Money

As you accumulate assets, your money tends to find its way into various investments, often in different places. You may have an IRA, funds left in an old 401(k), small bank accounts at several different banks, and money you inherited but never touched. These buckets are often ignored and occasionally forgotten. You pay little, if any attention to them, yet they could be producing more for you if you deposited them into an FIA or MYGA. Look around and see if you have any ignored buckets stashed away or gathering dust. If you do, consider putting them to work in an annuity.

CD Purchases or Coming Due Buckets

Most people own CDs and purchase them to keep their money safe while earning a decent return. Although CD rates are improving, they are still quite low, barely keeping up with inflation, if at all. Because MYGAs are like CDs in

CD Purchases or Coming Due

that they provide a guaranteed interest return over a selected period of time, many people use them as a CD alternative. Plus, MYGAs typically provide much higher interest rates than CDs.

Five-year MYGAs are paying up to 4.0% compared to five-year CDs, which currently yield about 3.1%. Additionally, since MYGAs are annuities, you don't have to pay taxes on the interest each year, as you do with CDs. That means you get extra return from the compounding effect of otherwise taxable funds remaining in the annuity. Remember, you are not taxed on an annuity until you take the funds out. If you have CDs coming due or are considering a CD purchase, check out MYGA rates. You will find that in most cases, they outperform the CD.

Excess Savings Buckets *(Includes Money Market Accounts)*

Excess Savings

It's important to have some money at hand in savings accounts to cover unexpected expenses. Over time, however, many people start to build up more savings than they really need, often without even realizing it. For example, many folks who must take their Required Minimum Distributions (RMDs) from their qualified funds don't need this money for income (which they have covered from other areas). Not knowing what to do with the RMDs, they deposit them in a savings account. Others may have received a bonus at work, saved more because they got an increase in salary, or inherited some money and don't know what to do with the extra cash. As time goes by, it's not uncommon to suddenly realize you have more savings than you really need and which are earning very little. It is these excess savings that may be suitable deposits into an MYGA or FIA.

Required Minimum Distributions

Required Minimum Distributions are funds that you are required to withdraw from your qualified accounts (IRA, 401(k), 403(b), TSA) once you turn 70½. Let's say that you don't need the RMD for income. If you're like most people and don't know what to do or where to invest these funds, they will find their way into a

Required Minimum Distributions (RMD)

savings or money market account. And there they sit, earning very little, and growing only as more deposits are made. If you are taking RMDs and you don't need income for expenses or have accumulated excess savings over the years from RMD deposits, a Fixed Index Annuity is a compelling alternative to risking these funds in the market.

Never Touch Money Buckets

Never Touch Money

You know that you will probably never need this money for future income, emergencies, or expenses. These are funds slated towards Growth Without Risk, perhaps for the benefit of heirs, or other purposes such as charity. If you are more conservative in nature and lean toward Growth Without Risk, consider placing these funds in an FIA that offers an enhanced death benefit. With an enhanced death benefit, when interest is credited to your annuity, an additional sum is added to a death benefit rider. Remember: this isn't a life insurance policy, just an enhanced death benefit option. So, there is no medical examination required—an important detail for people who have legacy money but cannot qualify for life insurance. This is a set-it-and-forget-it strategy where you know this part of your legacy will grow at a reasonable rate, at an enhanced rate with the death benefit, and without risk.

What's the Best Way to Select an Annuity?

You've decided that a Fixed Annuity is for you. Now the fun starts—selecting the annuity that has all the ingredients you need to reach your goals. To be candid, there are hundreds of annuities on the market, each with its own pros and cons. Trying to get all the information about these annuities and then sifting through each one to see if it's a good match is a daunting task. Here's where you will need the help of a professional who, once you've determined the goal of your annuity, will help you decide which is best for your circumstances.

When you meet with a professional, he or she will start by walking you through three core decisions that will narrow down your choices:

1. **What do you want:**
   - A MYGA which offers a guaranteed interest rate for a set number of years.
   - An FIA focused on growth.
   - An FIA focused on income.

2. **What length of annuity suits your needs:**
   - A shorter-term FIA (5-7 years).
   - A longer-term FIA (8 – 10 years).*

(*We do not recommend annuities with surrender periods longer than 10 years.)

3. **If you want income, what type of income will work for you:**
   - An FIA that offers a guaranteed roll-up followed by level income for life.
   - An FIA that offers a variable roll-up and an income that rises over time as your annuity earns interest.

Once these three core decisions are made, you will be able to dig deeper and evaluate the remaining choices about about such things as fees, crediting strategies, renewal rates, bonuses, company ratings, penalty-free withdrawal rates, nursing home or home healthcare benefits, death benefits and more.

Even if you work with a professional—hopefully a Fiduciary—you will find that no one annuity is perfect and that they all have their benefits and drawbacks. Your job, and the job of the person assisting you, is to talk through each feature and benefit of the annuity and evaluate how important that benefit is to you. At the end of the day, you must choose an annuity that you believe will serve you well and that won't stress you out after you purchase it.

Ultimately, your decision to purchase an annuity should give you peace of mind—otherwise, don't buy it!

Annuities: Yea or Nay?

At this point, you've been through each section of *1-2-3 Annuities*—"Discover," "Discuss," and now the last section, "Decide." If you recall, at the very beginning of our book, we looked at your Unique Annuity Mindset to determine your preconceptions about annuities. The sole purpose of *1-2-3 Annuities* is to provide objective information and perspective that will assist you in making a wise decision about these products. So, what's your Unique Annuity Mindset saying to you now? Take a few moments and answer the following questions with a "yea" or "nay" and let's find out.

Should I Own an Annuity?	Yea or Nay?
1 I worry about stock market volatility and I'd like to have a better balance of risk and safety.	Yea Nay
2 I have buckets of money that are not getting attention or just sitting there doing nothing or earning very little (cash, low interest CDs or similar).	Yea Nay
3 I want to make sure that my important expenses i.e. fixed expenses, insurance premiums, property taxes, utilities, etc., are 100% covered by guaranteed income.	Yea Nay
4 I like the idea of having more guaranteed income than provided by my Social Security and/or pension.	Yea Nay
5 I would prefer to forgo a little upside growth potential in exchange for no downside risk.	Yea Nay
6 I want to have a retirement income that I can't outlive— no matter what age I live to—and that rises to offset inflation.	Yea Nay
7 I believed that having a portion of money that is guaranteed not to lose principal will give me greater peace of mind and security.	Yea Nay
8 I'd like to take earn more money in the market, but I need a stronger non-correlated asset to hedge or cushion my overall portfolio risk / losses.	Yea Nay

Now, add up the yeas and nays. Ben Franklin used to say that the best way to make a decision is to add up the pros and cons, or the yeas and nays, and compare the totals. If the yeas outweigh the nays than you should move forward on your decision. If on the other hand, the nays outweigh the yeas, then you should pass. But in reality, it is still not that simple. You may find that one of the nays is so meaningful to you that it outweighs all the yeas.

If that's the case it would probably be best to slow down and make your decision after you've had a chance to review your feelings and goals. Remember, work at your pace to ensure that the decision is right for you and to make certain you are doing right by yourself and your family.

Conclusion

Are annuities for everyone? Certainly not!

Are annuities for you?

Well, we don't know. But we hope that your three-step journey through "Discover," "Discuss," and "Decide" has prepared you to determine whether an annuity is a good fit for you. If you have decided that an annuity may serve you well, your journey does not end here. Now, the challenge is finding the right annuity and the right person or company to work with.

Many people ask if they should work with someone in person or it is okay to work with someone long-distance. If you ask the right questions and feel confident that the person you are speaking with, either in person or on the telephone is out for your best interests, either way will work well for you.

The advantage of working in person is that you get to 'press the flesh' with him or her, which may make you feel more secure that that is the right person for you. On the other hand, if you work remotely, you should receive information via mail or email that gives you background on the person you're working with and the company he or she works for. And, if that person doesn't offer you face-to-face meetings via Skype or some other service, don't hesitate to ask for one.

Keep in mind that each agent, whether in person or from a website, will have a different personality and style of presenting to you. We recommend, however, that if you ever get the feeling that this person is trying to 'sell' you a specific annuity, or if you feel pressure from that person to 'buy now', that you should go look to work with someone else who is more aligned with your interests.

To assist your search, try using this questionnaire. You will find it a valuable ally which will help guide your buying process.

	My Annuity Questionnaire	1-2-3 Annuity Comments
1	Do you uphold the Fiduciary standard in writing?	*Only work with someone who is required to do so or who will put so in writing.*
2	Do most of your clients include annuities as part of their portfolio makeup?	*Only work with an advisor who regularly includes annuities in his/her planning.*
3	Are most of the annuities you employ Variable Annuities or Fixed Annuities?	*Shy away from Variable Annuities. Too many fees and no clear advantage over Fixed Annuities.*
4	Is this a Fixed Interest Annuity (MYGA) or a Fixed Index Annuity (FIA) we are talking about?	*They work differently. Be clear about the difference.*
5	What is the rating of the company for the annuity you are recommending?	*Stay in the "A" category.*

6	What is the length of the contract?	*Stay under 10 years.*
7	How much and when may I take funds from this annuity each year penalty free?	*Stick, for the most part, with annuities that offer 10% Penalty Free Withdrawals and allow for withdrawals for Required Minimum Distributions (RMD).*
8	Can I take my money out as a lump-sum at the end of the term of the contract?	*Never buy an annuity where you can't get your money out as a lump-sum.*
9	Is this an income focused or a growth focused annuity?	*Make sure you are focusing on what you want.*
10	If income focused, does it provide level income or rising income for life?	*Big difference, each with its own set of pros and cons. But we prefer rising income.*
11	When can I start taking income?	*Be careful, you may need income before the annuity permits it.*
12	Do I have to annuitize to get income or is the income considered a withdrawal from an Income Rider?	*Annuitization means you lose control of your principal. Be careful here. We almost always recommend an Income Rider.*
13	Does this annuity have any out of pocket fees other than Surrender Charges?	*Get the fees in writing to be clear.*
14	Are there nursing home or terminal illness benefits associated with this annuity?	*You may need the extra money.*
15	What Crediting Strategies are available?	*Ensure your annuity offers a variety of uncapped strategies.*

16	What stock market indices does this annuity link to?	*Avoid annuities with exotic or newer, unproven indexes.*
17	What does the surrender charge schedule look like? Does it decrease each year?	*Avoid annuities with high surrender charges that don't decrease for the first 4 – 5 years of the contract.*
18	Does this annuity offer a shorter version?	*Some annuities offer a shorter version (i.e. 6 years vs 10) with only minor differences.*
19	Are you a captive or independent insurance agent?	*Avoid captive agents as they may not show you all options.*
20	What is the commission on the products you're showing me?	*If you want to ask, ask. Don't feel it needs to be secret.*

So, that's the end of our journey through the world of annuities. As we said in the beginning, *1-2-3 Annuities* was written to help you cut through the noise circulating about annuities—the half-truths, untruths, biased and self-promoting reviews—so that you can make an intelligent, informed and accurate decision about this product class. Either way, yea or nay, we hope that we have fulfilled our mission!

Your Next Steps

If you're like many of our readers, you may still have questions that are more personal to your situation. We invite you to let us know how we can help. You may be considering a specific annuity and want to get a second opinion. Perhaps, you own annuities, but would like clarification about how they work and what benefits they offer. Or you might have older annuities that are coming due and you'd like to learn your best options, whether to keep the annuity you have or move it into something better. And, finally, because there are so many income options, you may find it helpful to let us walk you through the pros and cons of each.

We are here to answer all your questions and address all your concerns. Just send us an email, or head to our website. Better yet, give us a call and speak to one of our annuity experts, and do so without any obligation whatsoever. We'd love to hear from you and are cheering for your financial and retirement success.

Steve and Gabriel Lewit are holistic financial planners who focus on creating sustainable retirement income. With a combined 42-years of experience, Steve and Gabriel's planning approach integrates a modern, research-based method of investing designed to increase your retirement income and maximize the security of that income.

By incorporating annuities as a component of their clients' financial plans, Steve and Gabriel find that their clients report a higher level of retirement satisfaction and a greater quality of life. This approach ensures that income lasts throughout retirement, assets are preserved, and a minimal amount of risk is taken.

In their practice, Steve and Gabriel advocate an Evidenced Based Investing approach, whereby independent research, rather than arbitrary theories or beliefs, serve as the basis for all investing decisions. They have lectured throughout the U.S. and Steve has been

Steve Lewit   Gabriel Lewit

published in *The Wall Street Journal, Financial Times, Forbes, U.S. News, Chicago Women*, as well as appearing on CNN and WGN.

Both Steve and Gabriel guide their clients as a Fiduciary—which means they always put their clients' best interests first, no matter what. In that light they strive for excellence through consistent research, study, and through developing a deep understanding of each client's financial and emotional needs.

Their holistic approach is based on their ultimate goal of being objective and unbiased; to make sure every client understands the pros and cons of each investment decision; and to fit all the pieces of their financial puzzle together—Investment, Income, Insurance, Annuities, Estate Planning, Tax Minimization, Social Security Maximization, Gifting, Healthcare Planning and more—so that they work together effectively and efficiently.

Made in the USA
San Bernardino, CA
02 August 2020